PUBLICATIONS OF THE TEXAS FOLKLORE SOCIETY

MODY C. BOATRIGHT, Editor
WILSON M. HUDSON, Associate Editor
ALLEN MAXWELL, Associate Editor

NUMBER XXVIII

Madstones and Twisters

XXVIII

PUBLISHED BY
SOUTHERN METHODIST UNIVERSITY PRESS
DALLAS

Madstones
and
Twisters

Edited by
MODY C. BOATRIGHT
WILSON M. HUDSON
ALLEN MAXWELL

SOUTHERN METHODIST UNIVERSITY PRESS

DALLAS, TEXAS

Preface

THE TITLE of the present volume, *Madstones and Twisters,* taken from two separate articles, indicates that the contents have a wide range instead of being concentrated on one theme or subject as have some of the past publications of the Texas Folklore Society. Yet the different parts of the book fit together.

The madstones that J. Frank Dobie writes about have their counterpart in the bezoar stones of ancient India, and some of Howard C. Key's twisters dipped down into Texas last spring. There are still people who believe that a madstone will take the poison out of a bite by a mad dog or a rattlesnake, and the devastating and freakish tricks of tornadoes will always make the front pages of the newspapers. For ages rabies and tornadoes have cast fear into the heart of man, and it is of course to be expected that each would give rise to a body of beliefs and lore among the folk. To a great extent the Pasteur treatment has freed man from his fear of rabies, so that the belief in madstones, or even the knowledge of them, will eventually disappear. At the end of his article Mr. Key promises that it may be possible, by means of recently developed scientific methods, to spot and break up tornadoes before they can become fully formed and strike at our cities and towns. If this promise is realized, stories about tornadoes and their whimsical doings will become things of the past too.

In examining American folklore from the point of view of a European, Reidar Th. Christiansen of the University of Oslo deals with the question of what happens to folk beliefs and practices when a people exchange one way of life for another. These old beliefs and practices tend to become weakened and eventually die out altogether, but some show a strong vitality and persist in the face of changed conditions in the new land. Where immigrants have kept to themselves in some remote spot or even in a city, the European folklorist now and then finds a tale or a song that has not been heard for generations in the old country. In a sense Mody Boatright's article complements Mr. Christiansen's. Since the turn of the century the old way of life in America has been largely replaced by a new way in which greater numbers of people live closer together, hear and read the same thing, and work for great business concerns. The thesis developed by Mr. Boatright is that folklore, contrary to the usual assumption, does exist in such a society. Newspapers and other mass media spread many stories and beliefs that are properly to be considered folklore. Though industrialization may drive out one kind of folklore, it gives rise to a folklore of its own, which should be but is not always recognized as such. The two oil tales told by Jim Rowden will serve to illustrate this point.

The lore of weather and of planting that used to be expressed and disseminated by the almanacs has been greatly weakened within recent times, though many people still believe that root crops are to be planted only when the moon is in the dark. Everett A. Gillis shows that there is much more of interest in the old almanacs than the prediction of weather and directions about when to plant. Almanacs have been put out of date by modern weather reports, which can be had almost hourly by any farmer with a radio or television set. Like almanacs, the prairie dogs of Lanvil Gilbert's article have seen their day. Once they were as numerous and as characteristic of the Great Plains as the buffalo, but they had to be killed off for the same reason, to make way for man's cattle.

Mexican lore is well represented by the articles contributed by Américo Paredes, Elton Miles, and Riley Aiken. Until recently the greater part of the *gente* along the Rio Grande and in the lower country have continued to live in the way of their fathers, and today many still do. There the old traditions are kept alive.

The last four items belong to a class that may be thought of as family lore—stories preserved by and told in a family. These stories may be recognized by the tellers as folktales or they may be thought of as true family history. It is, of course, very difficult to say that what comes out of a family storehouse is or is not true. Ad Lawrence's tale about the mule on the buffalo hunt contains nothing hard to believe, but it is practically identical with a tale told by John C. Duval in *The Young Explorers* (first published in *Burke's Weekly*, 1870-71). Lawrence located his hunt south of the San Gabriel and Duval his south of the Brushy, only a few miles away; the hunters are not the same men, but what happens is the same. It is possible that we may have here what Mr. Dobie has called "the traveling anecdote," which may be transferred freely from one historical person to another. Even when a story is not borrowed entire with a change of names, a given family story tends to take on a pattern pleasing to the folk mind and hence to resemble in a general way stories told by other families. That there is true history in such stories must be admitted; and let us admit further that when we stand in "the shadow of history" we cannot clearly distinguish real events from imaginary ones.

The editors take this opportunity to invite members of the Texas Folklore Society and other readers of this volume to write down and send in the stories belonging to their families. Material is now being collected for the next annual publication.

MODY C. BOATRIGHT
WILSON M. HUDSON
ALLEN MAXWELL

Austin and Dallas
March 8, 1958

Contents

Madstones and Twisters

Madstones and Hydrophobia Skunks

J. FRANK DOBIE

THE MADSTONE, in a way, is a symbol of mankind's enduring credulity, which never turns loose of one phantom without grabbing onto another. Like the world's chief religions, it had its origins in the Orient and in magic. The tourist-patronized snake charmer of India—descended by birth from centuries of professionals—insures himself against a possible cobra bite by carrying (1) a root supposed to have such powerful emetic and purgative effects that it will rid the blood system of venom and (2) a black stone potent in absorbing poison from any snake bite to which it is applied. This stone is reputed to be spewed out of a toad buried alive. Its properties are magic, like those of the ancient bezoar stone, which was used to defend princes against poison and to call floods down upon enemy armies. The bezoar stone appears to have been the primary antecedent of the recently modern madstone.[1]

A scholar might write a long lucubration—perhaps some scholar has already written it—on the relation of madstones to the amulets, periapts, talismans, and kindred charms in which the Persians were surpassingly opulent. As Sir Walter Scott relates in his introduction and also in a note to *The Talisman*, the magic amulet giving that novel its title became, centuries after a Crusader had gained it from a Saracen and brought it back to Scotland, "restricted" in its uses "to the cure of persons bitten by mad dogs." The stone, set in silver, became a noted heirloom at the seat of Lee in Clydesdale. In the eighteenth century a Presbyterian Assembly at Glasgow, which is also in Clydesdale, debated on the "superstitious using of the stone for the curing of deseased Cattle," which drank water into which it had been "cast." The Assembly concluded that since no words "such as Sorcereirs use" accompanied treatment by the stone and since it had "pleast God to give to stones and herbs a special vertue for healing of many infirmities in man and beast," the Laird of Lee might go on getting virtue out of the Lee Stone.

By the time madstones became popular in America, more in the South and Southwest than elsewhere, the magic element had almost entirely vanished from them. The power to suck poison from flesh and absorb it that believers ascribed to the madstone was, for them, in the same category of physical laws as action of a suction pump. The talisman, brought back by Crusaders who had dedicated their lives to the Holy Land, held within itself unfathomable mysteries of the East, propitious properties from On High, communicable charms from some other Unknowable. The disappearance of its supernaturalities through a shift in credulity but prefigured the descent of a God too awful, majestical, and spiritual for human comprehension to the Silent Partner that businessmen now credit for their success in the pursuit of greed—which, of course, they call something else.

Bezoar stones, Belgium black stones, elk stones, buffalo stones, Indian stones, snake-stones, madstones, and their congeners generally came out of the bodies of animals. One kind of snake-stone of Bengal is said to be found "within the head of the adjutant bird,"[2] but in that delightful book, *Beast and Man in India*, John Lockwood Kipling (father of Rudyard) describes the snake-stone as "a porous piece of calcined bone, pumice-stone, or something of that nature." The Ayr Stone of Scotland was originally used for whetting knives, but somebody, it seems, somewhere professed it effective in drawing snake poison from a wound and so it became another snake-stone. A man in Texas, both sincere and set in his ignorance, once displayed to me a chunk of lava as a madstone. "Can't get a redbird, bluebird'll do." The serpent-stone—called "Chinese stone" on account of its having come to Mexico from the Philippines—used by eighteenth-century Indians in Lower California was burnt deer horn, though cheats palmed off burnt ox bone for the real thing.[3] One scholar identifies ancient bezoar stones as kidney or gall stones, but—with few exceptions—the most valued and historic madstones of recent times in the United States came from the stomachs of ruminants.

As a boy, I found a "stone" that had been carried by a fat cow butchered on our ranch in Live Oak County, Texas. The grass-filled stomach, intestines, and lights of the animal had been dragged some distance away from the butchering place and left on the ground. During the following night coyotes had made merry with the fleshy parts of the refuse, and when the next morning I came by the scattered heap of undigested grass out of the stomach I saw the "stone." In shape it was a flattened ball, maybe two inches in diameter, but not more than half that thick. A smooth, speckled-gray, permeable covering of calcium enclosed a compact mass of material that looked like hairs and moss fiber. Not long after this I saw a dried-up and cracked-open "stone" of the same kind near the bleached bones of a cow brute that had died on the range. There must not have been much demand for madstones in our part of the country at the time; I do not recall much talk of them, but I do recall that some people thought that every cow had such a "stone" as I have described for use as a cud. They supposed that a contented cow would belch up her cud and chew on it for pleasure, very much as people chew gum.

People who knew the most about madstones knew that the best ones came out of the stomachs of white deer. No stone out of a cow could have the virtue of one out of a deer. The deer that had a stone was not always white, but whiteness in a carrier gave the stone more drawing power. Some scien-

tifically inclined people suggested that the stone depleted the
strength of a deer carrying it and had something to do with
the white hairs. One time I saw a white deer, a doe, on the
King Ranch. I was with Mr. Caesar Kleberg, a manager, and
suggested that the deer be shot and examined for a madstone;
he was really more scientific-natured than I am but was not
interested in madstones.

It is mostly of madstones applied like leeches to the bites
of "hydrophobia cats" and the like that this essay treats, but
before we settle down on ranges where the cowboys, the deer
and the antelope play, I want to quote from fantastic Thomas
Falkner, the English Jesuit who went to the Argentine about
1730 and missionaried among the Indians. In that country,
he recorded,

there are considerable quantities of the occidental bezoar, found not only
in the stomach of the guanacoes and vicunias, but also of the anta [tapir]
.... When it is given in a considerable quantity, it greatly promotes a
diaphoresis. I have almost always found it give relief and immediate ease
in heartburns, faintings, etc., the dose consisting of a dram, or two
scruples, taken in anything; though it might be given in larger quantity
with great safety. I have found it preferable, in many cases, to our
testaceous powders and mineral substances. I have had some of these
stones that weighed eighteen ounces each.[4]

Until the researches of Louis Pasteur led, in 1885, to successful inoculation against rabies, there was no sure way to
prevent a person infected with the rabies virus from succumb-
ing to hydrophobia. Of course, not every bitten person suc-
cumbed. In fact, according to science, between 80 and 85
per cent of human beings may escape infection from the virus.
Even with that knowledge mighty few people bitten by an
animal either rabid or potentially rabid want to risk not being
immune. In pre-Pasteur days, the one hope of being saved
from a malady more horrible in its manifestations than any
other on earth was to get to a madstone. Up to 80 per cent
of the patients could not go mad, on account of natural immunity. The madstone got credit for that. It took years for

Pasteur's science to supplant the theory and application of madstones. A Pasteur Institute for detection of the rabies virus and for treatment of victims was not established in Texas, at Austin, until 1903.

The stone was moistened in warm milk—water could not be trusted—and applied to a wound. If it did not adhere, the person being treated was presumed not to have the virus. To do any good, it had to stick to the flesh for a long while, drawing the poison out of the wound and absorbing it into its own porous substance. After it had soaked up a certain amount of poison it would no longer adhere. Then it would be put into a vessel of warm or hot milk, and the milk would turn green from the poison being released by the madstone. Some opera- tors let the milk boil and considered the thumping of the madstone on the bottom of the vessel a good sign. Its pores having been cleansed, it would be applied again to the wound until it no longer adhered.

It was as effective in drawing out snake venom as venom from a rabid animal, but victims of snakebite were seldom within reach of a madstone when bitten, could not wait to get to one, and had to resort to whiskey or some other remedy. Steve Heffington, tax assessor and collector of Travis County, Texas, tells me that when he was a boy at the turn of the century a madstone owned by George Johnson on Cypress Creek, in that county, was even used to draw the poison out of wasp stings—if nobody bitten by a snake or a mad dog were using it.

It was generally considered that a person infected with rabies could not go mad for at least two weeks. (Actually the average period of virus incubation varies from forty to sixty days.) Even in the horse age there was time for a victim to ride hundreds of miles to a madstone. Thomas Carson, a Scot who began ranching in Arizona in 1883 and in the next decade acquired an enormous ranch in New Mexico, later wrote: "A skunk-bitten man at once starts off for Texas, where at certain

places one can hire the use of a madstone."[5] A cowboy of the
Texas Panhandle might take a train for Kansas City.[6] A dispatch
from Gainesville, Texas, dated April 29, and printed in the
Galveston *Daily News* of May 3, 1879, reads: "A man in town
yesterday from the Pan Handle said he had been bitten by a
mad dog and had ridden 350 miles in four days and nights,
coming to a mad stone [here]. The stone stuck nine times."

In *No Life for a Lady*—worth all the other books written
by women on ranch life, plus a few hundred written by men
—Agnes Morley Cleaveland vivifies "a haggard-looking man on
a haggard-looking horse" riding up to her ranch, out from
Magdalena, New Mexico, jerking off his hat, showing her two
red marks next to the hairline on his forehead, and announcing,
"A hybie-phobie skunk bit me. . . . They say there's a madstone
in Socorro! If I can git to it in time! I've been on this horse
twenty hours already. He can't make it on."

He drank a cup of coffee, slept two hours while competent
Miss Agnes rustled up the remuda and saddled him a fresh
horse. Then he rode on. Returning a few days later, he jubi-
lantly described how the milk-soaked madstone had "pulled"
the poison out of his head and, after it had discharged its
accumulation of green venom in milk, kept on pulling until
there wasn't any poison left to pull.[7]

Skunk bites probably spurred more riding to madstones in
the Southwest than bites from dogs, coyotes, and other animals.
Any wild animal that bit a person not cornering it was supposed, not without reason, to be mad. It seems that over a
considerable span of years skunks outdid any other species in
biting campers. These little varmints were usually called pole-
cats, though the polecat is not native to America, is not a musk-
carrier, and is no more of a cat than the skunk is. They were
also called "hydrophobia cats" and "hydrophobia skunks." The
spotted skunk—called also "civet cat"—was singled out from
the other two species (the striped skunk and the hog-nosed
skunk) as being especially active in biting. I suppose it was a

striped skunk that bit a Mexican girl named Lupe, a house servant on our ranch, one night while she was sleeping on a pallet on the floor of an open hallway. It bit her on the toe, but when she reacted it left the premises. I was a child at the time and remember that while there was some talk of hydrophobia there was no pilgrimage to a madstone. My mother poulticed the bite, not severe, with fat bacon and Lupe suffered no ill effects.

Belief in hydrophobia skunks must be understood in order to appreciate a relation made to me in 1929 by a noted frontiersman of Texas named Andy Mather. He was at his home in Liberty Hill, Williamson County, when I visited him, full of recollections about mustangs, buffaloes, madstones, and other vanished forms of life.

In a year before barbed wire "played hell with Texas," he said, he was with an outfit of about twenty-five men working cattle in the Devil's River country. They reached Pecan Springs away after dark with a herd of cattle, some of which had not had water for three days. Horses, cattle, and men were all played out. The boss said to turn the herd loose. It was summer and the men unsaddled their horses among scattering trees, staked them out, and lay down on their saddles for pillows.

Lying a step or two away from Andy Mather was a man named Perrin. Along in the night Mather was awakened by a great commotion. When he raised up he saw in the clear starlight Perrin struggling with a "polecat" that had him by the nose while he was pulling fiercely to loosen its hold. When Perrin got it loose, he threw it to the ground with such force that the animal was killed. His nose was badly torn. The "polecat" had not emitted any odoriferous fluid, and this was taken as a sure sign that it was mad. Perrin was considerably excited over the prospect of suffering the most horrible of all forms of death.

Somebody said that the Bradford family at Menard had a

madstone. Perrin got on the freshest horse in the outfit and set out at once for Menard, about 125 miles away. As Andy Mather learned later, Perrin reached the madstone and had the satisfaction of seeing it adhere to his torn nose. It drew out a lot of poison, as the green color it gave the milk in which it was soaked showed. Perrin got all right, and he did not go mad.

There were two signs of rabies in a biting skunk: it would not loose its hold and it gave off no odor. In 1939 an ex-cowboy of the Staked Plains named V. Whitlock, then living at Beaumont, Texas, gave me the following account in manuscript form:

> My brother and I was staying in camp, up on the Plains, sleeping on the ground in a tent. One night he awaked me and told me to light the lantern, that something had hold of him. When I lighted the lantern I saw a polecat with its teeth fastened in my brother's scalp with a death grip. He had the cat around the neck with both hands, also in a death grip.
>
> We had to pull its hold out by main strength, and then I held it up by its tail and broke its neck with a branding iron. My brother did not wait till daylight to saddle his horse and ride for the nearest railroad station to catch a train for Toyah, Texas, where a man owned a madstone. . . . It stuck to his wound about twelve hours before it released its hold. The poison was boiled out of it twice before it quit sticking. My brother suffered no ill effects from the bite.

Only a few months after Andy Mather told me of the "polecat" bite in a cow camp and the victim's ride to the Bradford madstone at Menard, I was in that town, on the San Saba River, and looked up George Bradford. He said that he remembered the cowboy named Perrin who rode from Devil's River to the madstone. The stone, however, had not belonged to him but to his wife's people, who were named Ellis. It had been brought to Texas from Tennessee, where Grandma Ellis' father found it in a deer's stomach early in the 1800's. He was a great hunter and always cut open the stomach of every deer he killed, looking for madstones. The deer from which he got this one was not white. Its stomach contained two madstones. He gave one of them away.

The one he kept and brought to Texas was about the size of a guinea egg, one side of it flattish. The flat surface was especially handy for applying to wounds. It was used to draw out rattlesnake poison as well as hydrophobia poison. People came to it from as far away as New Mexico. It was kept in a trunk with other valuables, and no matter how hard and brittle its surface looked to be, as soon as it was soaked in warm milk it became porous, ready to draw poison into itself.

The San Saba River flood of 1900 got up into the Ellis home and washed away the trunk and many other belongings. The trunk was later found on the riverbank miles below Menard. Some of the contents had been spilled out where the trunk lodged, but the madstone was not among them, nor was it in the trunk. The last time any of the family saw it was not long before the flood, when two strangers came to view it. They acted rather peculiarly and handled the madstone for such a long time that the owner grew tired of staying with them and told them to put it back in the trunk when they were through with it. A year or two after the flood a man from Menard who knew the Ellises very well and was familiar with their madstone met two men in Arizona displaying one that looked exactly like it. He recollected having seen the men in Menard. High enough prices were sometimes paid for madstones to make them worth stealing.

Certain madstones, like the Lockett Stone and the Pointer Stone of Virginia, were kept in the hands of plantation owners for generations.[8] An heired sword could not be divided, but an heired madstone could. Collin McKinney of Kentucky settled in Texas in time to sign the Declaration of Independence from Mexico, after which he served in the Congress of the Republic and had Collin County named after him. The famous Ben Milam, also from Kentucky, who was in Texas before any legalized colonists arrived from the United States, thought enough of McKinney to present him with a third of a madstone "about the size of a goose egg."

The history of this madstone, based on two newspaper articles[9] published long after "Old Ben Milam" was killed at the storming of San Antonio in 1835, is clouded. According to one account, Milam brought it with him when he came to Texas; according to the other, it was "found on a beach." Ben Milam had been on plenty of beaches. I myself have seen water-cut porous stones, which I judged to be of lava, on beaches fronting the Gulf of Mexico. The part of his madstone, whatever its origin, that Ben Milam kept was lost in fire that destroyed his home. Before Collin McKinney died in 1861, he divided his part of the Milam Stone into enough pieces for each of his children to have a precious sliver.

A son in Collin County in 1875 had a piece only about half an inch square, but it was still drawing poison out of flesh bitten by rabid animals. This McKinney son claimed that during forty-seven years as a family possession the stone had saved four hundred people from hydrophobia and had failed to work on only two. One of them was already having convulsions when the stone was applied to his wound; the other had so many whiskers on his chin, where the bite had been made, that the stone could not adhere. Presumably the man of whiskers preferred hydrophobia to shaving; not long after the madstone failed to draw out the poison through his whiskers, he went into the horrible convulsions of hydrophobia.

I have never heard of an owner of a madstone who charged outrageously for the use of it. In 1875, one W. M. James of Fannin County was bitten on the leg by a mad dog loose on the streets of Sherman. He rode at once to the McKinney farm in Collin County. The madstone "refused to take hold," and then the leg began to swell and Mr. James to suffer from an "unnatural headache." Again the madstone—this piece out of the original Ben Milam Stone—was applied. It adhered to the wound and at once began drawing. For thirty-one hours, during which time it dropped off four times and was four times relieved of its surfeit of poison by being soaked in hot milk, it sucked poison out of the leg until not a tincture remained. The shrines of Guadalupe in Mexico and of Lourdes in France never did better. McKinney charged Mr. James only $3.00 for taking care of him and his horse for three days and letting the madstone cure him besides.

A generous-natured woman in Van Horn, Texas, had a light-colored, porous stone, supposed to have come off the bottom of a sailing ship, that would suck hydrophobia virus out of any wound to which it was applied. Jim Roberts, manager for the big Gage ranches in West Texas, while sleeping in camp one night was bitten on the forehead by a "hydrophobia cat," a skunk. It took him three days to ride horseback to Van Horn, but when he got there the madstone stuck to his wound like a horseshoe to a magnet, for twenty-five minutes. He was never touched by hydrophobia.[10]

While expressing scientific doubt of madstones, Judge C. V. Terrell of Austin tells[11] of an experience with one. When he was twelve years old, at Decatur, Texas, in 1873, a house cat bit him on his left knee and then when he knocked it off with his right hand bit him on the wrist. The cat, beyond all doubt, had hydrophobia. It bit several dogs; one of them went mad and bit a cow that went mad. It also bit a carpenter in the calf of his leg and about two weeks later he died of hydrophobia.

Judge Terrell's father called in the family doctor. The doctor advised cutting off the boy's right hand, including the cat-bitten wrist. When the father called attention to the fact that the boy had been bitten on the knee as well as on the wrist, the doctor said there was no cure for hydrophobia.

But someone told Mr. Terrell of a man named Ab Stepp, living near the mouth of Oliver Creek in Denton County, who possessed a madstone. Terrell drove his wounded son in a buggy to the Stepp homestead. To quote Judge Terrell's own words:

We got to the place about noon. I went to bed and Stepp took my wrist, scarified it and applied a small porous stone about three fourths of an inch long and about half an inch through each way. He would let it remain on the wound for half an hour or more and would then take it off and soak it for a while in a cup of warm sweet milk. Just before dark the stone seemed to adhere no longer to the wound. Stepp said that all the poison had been drawn out. He now began applying the stone to the cat bite on my knee. About one o'clock that night the stone quit adhering and Stepp said to go to sleep. The next morning my father paid him $25 and we returned home. We were all uneasy for a long time, but no sign of hydrophobia ever showed up in my system. My brother John was one of the prime movers in establishing the Pasteur treatment for rabies here in Austin.

People used to city life with all its mechanical and scientific devices for the body's health and comfort must employ the transporting power of imagination to realize the utter helplessness of a human being away out in the country bitten by a mad animal or a poisonous snake—and also the wish to be helpful by somebody possessing a madstone. In 1955, W. F. Kahlden of Houston, who was born in 1874, sent me the following account:

We were farming in Fayette County, Texas, when at the age of seven I was bitten on the toe by a water moccasin. I ran as fast as I could to the house and told my mother. She called a field hand and told him to take me to the house of a poor Indian about a mile away who had what people called the Indian Madstone. His name was Clem Knowles. People would come to him from far away with all kinds of infections and bites to be treated. He never asked for pay and provided food and shelter free to whoever came. He may have been ignorant, but he was generous and kind-hearted.

The field hand did not take time to get a horse but started walking with me to the Indian Madstone. By the time we had gone half a mile my leg and foot were so swollen that I could no longer walk. The field hand took me up in his arms and carried me on. The first thing Clem Knowles did was to give me some whiskey. Then he slit my toe at the bite. The Indian Madstone was already heating in milk. It was porous, no bigger than a thimble and flat at one end. He placed the flat surface against the wound and it adhered until it was full of poisonous matter. When he boiled it, poisonous-looking bubbles came to the surface. He kept applying the stone until it refused to draw any more. It was thirty days before I could walk, and a black band showed around my waist for years, but I recovered fully from a very poisonous bite.

Most doctors would say that the patient would have recovered sooner without any madstone treatment if he had not run and walked so much following the bite. The remedies that doctors before Pasteur had for hydrophobia were no more valid scientifically than the madstone treatment. Some acceded to the madstone; some did not. Dr. C. C. Black of Georgetown, Texas, told me early in this century that he knew a man in the county who would not have a doctor for his baby bitten by a mad dog but took it to a madstone. Not long after the treatment he proudly told Dr. Black that the stone had "stuck six times." Six weeks later the baby died of hydrophobia.

In the way that certain old-time hard cases turned to God at the end of their power to go on sinning, some people turned to madstones; they might not believe fully, but there wasn't anything else at all to believe in. According to his law partner and biographer, W. H. Herndon, Abraham Lincoln said that faith in madstones "looked like a superstition" but that belief in them by country people based on "actual experiment" made him accept it. Like madstones, much attributed to Lincoln is folklore. Albert Beveridge, following Herndon, cited testimony that Lincoln took his son Robert, after he had been bitten by a dog, to a madstone at Terre Haute, Indiana. The way an Indiana doctor I know heard it, Lincoln's father took him, as a boy, to a stone at Brazil, Indiana. Well, Brazil isn't far from Terre Haute. Faith of our fathers—

Cowboy talk on the subject overheard by Owen Wister in Wyoming and fancied up for fiction illustrates the final farce that all sorts of "faiths" can be brought to. The following extract is from Wister's *The Virginian,* published in 1902:

"Speakin' of bites," spoke up a new man, "how's that?" He held up his thumb.
"My!" breathed Scipio. "Must have been a lion."
The man wore a wounded look. "I was huntin' owl eggs for a

botanist from Boston," he explained.... "The young feller wore knee-pants and ever so thick spectacles with a half-moon cut in 'em. . . . Well, he would have owl eggs—them little prairie-owl that some claim can turn their head clean around and keep a-watchin' yu', only that's non-sense. We was ridin' through that prairie-dog town, used to be on the flat just after yu' crossed the south fork of Powder River on the Buffalo trail, and I said I'd dig an owl nest out for him if he was willin' to camp till I'd dug it. I wanted to know about them owls myself—if they did live with the dogs and snakes. . . .

"So while the botanist went glarin' around the town with his glasses to see if he could spot a prairie-dog and an owl usin' the same hole, I was diggin' a hole I'd seen an owl run down. And that's what I got." He held up his thumb again.

"The snake!" I exclaimed.

"Yes, sir. Mr. Rattler was keepin' house that day. Took me right there. I hauled him out of the hole hangin' to me. Eight rattles."

"Eight!" said I. "A big one."

"Yes, sir. Thought I was dead. But the woman—"

"The woman?" said I.

"Yes, woman. Didn't I tell yu' the botanist had his wife along? Well, he did. And she acted better than the man, for he was losin' his head, and shoutin' he had no whiskey, and he didn't guess his knife was sharp enough to amputate my thumb, and none of us chewed, and the doctor was twenty miles away, and if he had only remembered to bring his ammonia—well, he was screeching out 'most everything he knew in the world, and without arranging it any, neither. But she just clawed his pocket and burrowed and kep' yelling, 'Give him the stone, Augustus!'

"And she whipped out one of them Injun medicine-stones,—first one I ever seen,—and she clapped it on to my thumb, and it started in right away."

"What did it do?" said I.

"Sucked. Like blotting-paper does. Soft and funny it was, and gray. They get 'em from elks' stomachs, yu' know. And when it had sucked the poison out of the wound, off it falls off my thumb by itself! And I thanked the woman for saving my life that capable and keeping her head that cool. I never knowed how excited she had been till afterward. She was awful shocked."

"I suppose she started to talk when the danger was over," said I, with deep silence around me.

"No; she didn't say nothing to me. But when her next child was born, it had eight rattles."

1. For some learning on the subject, see "Bezoar Stones," by George Gaylord Simpson, in *Natural History Magazine,* XL (October, 1937),

599-602. In an article, "Snakes Are Show Biz in India," by Peggy and Pierre Streit, *New York Times Magazine*, July 21, 1957, Prime Minister Nehru is quoted as remarking that the snake charmers "seem to satisfy the intelligence of tourists."

2. Thomas Carson, *Ranching, Sport and Travel* (London, 1911), p. 33.

3. Francisco Javier Clavigero, *The History of Lower California*, trans. and ed. Sara E. Lake and A. A. Gray (Palo Alto: Stanford University Press, 1937), pp. 393-95.

4. Thomas Falkner, *A Description of Patagonia and the Adjoining Parts of South America* (1774), ed. Arthur E. S. Neumann (Chicago, 1935), p. 89.

5. Carson, *op. cit.*, pp. 112-13.

6. Reginald Aldridge, *Ranch Notes* (London, 1884), p. 194.

7. Agnes Morley Cleaveland, *No Life for a Lady* (Boston, 1941), pp. 148-49.

8. Joseph Blunt Cheshire, *Nonnula* (Chapel Hill: University of North Carolina Press, 1930), pp. 204-10.

9. One article, attributed to the *Texas Republican* of June 4, 1869, is quoted in Dr. Pat Ireland Nixon's *A Century of Medicine in San Antonio* (San Antonio, 1936), p. 109; the other is from the Dallas *Weekly Herald*, May 22, 1875.

10. Frost Woodhull, "Ranch Remedios," in *Man, Bird, and Beast*, ed. J. Frank Dobie ("Publications of the Texas Folklore Society," VIII; Austin, 1930), p. 24.

11. C. V. Terrell, *The Terrells: Eighty-Five Years, Texas from Indians to Atomic Bombs* (Austin, 1948), pp. 100-101.

A European Folklorist
Looks at American Folklore

REIDAR TH. CHRISTIANSEN

Address to the Texas Folklore Society, April 13, 1957

THE VERY CHOICE of a subject like this may seem slightly presumptuous, especially to the distinguished company of Texas folklorists whose collections and studies, accessible in many books and papers, have been one of the most stimulating discoveries to a student coming from the northwestern corner of Europe. He comes from a country which in most ways is very different from your own, a country where folk tradition had been formed and determined by a different national history, as by different geographical conditions. Accordingly, his conception of folklore would naturally be colored by his knowledge of the folklore of his own country. As a preface he therefore wants to state that his intention in no way was to talk about American folklore per se. What he wanted to do was to give an impression of what the great discovery of American folklore has been to him personally, and further to state, and explain, his conviction of the great importance that this new province of folklore has had for the study of European folklore and for folklore studies in general.

At the outset one has to realize what is the general impression most Europeans have of things American, and their conclusion, sometimes openly stated, that the term "American folklore" is self-contradictory. The reason may well be that folklore, or whatever term may be preferred, seems to evoke certain associations with something ancient like a ballad, beautiful and simple; with something witty and pointed like

18

a folktale or a proverb; or with something unreasonable, sometimes to the point of being frightening, like an item of folk belief or of ancient custom. Not necessarily silly, however, because there is always present a sense of continuity, of familiarity, that makes people look at folklore items with a kind of recognition and inner understanding, however vague. But the general idea of America and things American held by the average European is that of an entirely new world, strangely uniform in character. With regard to Latin America, his ideas are more vague still, to the extent that he may be said to be almost totally unaware of its existence. To a Scandinavian at all events, America primarily means the United States, in later years perhaps also Canada—the countries to which his countrymen, in a number exceeding that of those who stayed home, emigrated, and where they settled, some of them to return, strangely changed, after many years. Accordingly, to most Scandinavians America is above all the "land of progress," a land where the heavy burdens of tradition, of history, of nationalism—as of social convention and classification—have been discarded, the very points stressed in the early pamphlets which advertised the newly opened land to prospective emigrants. The idea of the land of wealth unlimited, the "world of perfection," to borrow a term coined by Priestley, is confirmed by the glittering advertisements in the countless magazines and papers through which the United States is presented to the common reading public. In a strange way other associations seemingly different are added to this brilliant, easygoing world; associations with elements daring and adventurous, with exploits, with never-ending opportunities of parading as hero and savior in conflicts with brute, evil forces of nature or of humanity. Such associations may to some extent be derived from youthful reminiscences of the world of Fenimore Cooper, the main source, however, being the films that in endless variety present to the public in every town, no matter how small, this strange world and thus account for the ever-growing popularity of cowboys, guns, and lone trails in a country where nothing of this kind ever did exist.

Such observations may explain why the existence in the New World of a folklore tradition closely related to the oral tradition current in their own country might appear foreign to European students.

When in 1888 the American Folklore Society began its activities and the first number of its journal was published, the editors stated their program (*JAFL*, I, 3-7) as the preservation of oral tradition mainly in four different fields: (a) relics of English folklore, (b) the traditions of the Negroes, (c) the lore of the Indian tribes, and (d) the folklore of French Canada and the Spanish Southwest. The main interest of a European folklorist will naturally be directed to the first and the fourth fields, i.e., to the fate of the European traditional heritage in America, including the folklore of various national groups of immigrants as well. He might want to add still another field, perhaps of even greater interest: the emergence of what one might call a new and characteristic type of genuine *American* folklore.

Proceeding with an attempt at a survey of what types of folklore may be expected to exist, the American Folklore Society's opening program declared: "As respects old ballads ... the prospect of obtaining much of value is not flattering. Still, genuine ballads continue to be sung in the colonies; a few have been recorded...." This was written in 1888, and now some seventy years later one need only refer to Tristram P. Coffin's *The British Traditional Ballad in North America* (1950) or to Marius Barbeau's collections and study of French folksongs in Canada to realize how far the "not flattering" prospects have been exceeded. From Coffin's bibliography one will see how rich the ballad material actually is, with American versions of popular ballads such as "Barbara Allen" or "Lady Isabel" far more numerous than are the known variants of the same ballads in Great Britain.

With regard to folktales the program stated: "For the collection of ancient nursery tales the prospects are more hopeful; scarcely a single such tale has been recorded in America, yet it is certain that, until within a very few years, they existed in great abundance.... There is reason to hope that some of these may be saved from oblivion." Even if ballad and song seem to have survived better, the international folktale is well represented, and a useful bibliography is available in the thesis of Ernest Warren Baughman, *A Comparative Study of the Folktales of England and North America* (1953) with a great number of additions from later publications and from the excellent notes added therein. The program then passed to what were called "superstitions," or let us rather say folk belief. "Superstitions ... survive in abundance. The belief in witchcraft lingers, not only in remote valleys in Virginia and Tennessee, but in the neighbourhood of Eastern cities. Faith in signs and omens, prejudices in respect to colors of dress and costume, belief in lucky days and inherited methods of work, continue in some measure to influence conduct." This statement, made seventy years ago, is of a certain interest because it seems to me that during the later decades it is folk belief and customs that are losing ground while tales and ballads survive far better. The reason probably is that the latter two are not as intimately connected with daily life, which has been increasingly modernized and has essentially changed in later periods. Fairly rich American materials have, however, been collected, consisting not only of such ideas as have a functional value in everyday life, or may "influence conduct" of people, but also of strange beliefs which often can be followed backward to European stories and legends of the Middle Ages. A good instance is the ancient belief that on Christmas Eve, even on "old" Christmas Eve, household animals have the power of speech, a belief recorded from various parts of the States, strangely remote from daily life, and founded solely on ancient tradition. Finally, the editor stresses the importance of recording such minor elements of folklore as proverbs, rhymes, riddles, and sayings, and of these he is certain a rich collection could still be made, as it obviously has been.

Without considering the rich field of Negro contributions to American folklore, or the still more extensive materials available for a study of the traditions of the American Indians, one may by now confidently assert that the materials for folklore studies are much more extensive than the founders assumed. The *Journal,* as only a casual glance at its *Index* will show, has made accessible, and is constantly adding to, a wealth of information and themes for an unlimited number of special studies. The field has grown so vast that every folklorist is ready to join in the hope expressed by the editors that the future will see the preparation of "a complete bibliography of American folklore, to which already belongs an extensive literature."

The discovery of American folklore as a colorful and important element in American life, and the means of augmenting its influence in studies as in revival of what is of value and picturesque, are matters on which a European folklorist can hardly offer any advice. To him, the main interest is connected with the fact that he in the New World is confronted with a traditional heritage, mainly derived from the same sources as is the oral tradition of his own country. His first reaction is a mingled surprise and gratitude at finding such considerable additions to the study of folklore. Until some years ago, the best known—perhaps the only—source was the book of the German Karl Knortz, the editor of a German daily in Indianapolis, and later the superintendent of German schools in Evansville, Indiana: *Streifzüge auf dem Gebiete der Amerikanischer Volkskunde* (1902). It was the first indication in print of the preservation of such things as proverbs, rhymes, and riddles. A special point of interest to a student of folklore, however, is the new access opened to the knowledge of the central problem, i.e., the transmission of folklore matter from one people to another, a problem always arising when a student is faced with the astounding similarity apparent everywhere in conceptions, and still more surprising, in the expression of these in words or in practice. Inevitably the next question is this: what happens to such folklore elements when they pass from one group to another, and how do they react to and combine with the advance of the international, modern type of life and civilization? American folklore presents materials of special value in the study of such problems. What happens to this complex of ideas and tales when they are transferred to entirely new surroundings? Studies of this kind lead further to more general problems such as the relationship between folklore elements and the milieu, their special characteristics and background, the dependence of the elements on a definite soil for their life or on special national or geographical conditions, and the readiness or reluctance of the elements to be transferred or volatilized. A priori one would be inclined to believe that the products of imagination—folktales and ballads —would have a far better chance of surviving a transfer than have elements more intimately bound up with the exigencies of daily life. Beliefs, customs, and legends that serve as an explanation or codification of folk conceptions associated with a certain way of living become weakened as this way yields to another.

On this point the difference is obvious between the attitude toward a traditional heritage possessed by the early settlers and pioneers, and that held by immigrants arriving at a later date, when American life had attained a definite pattern. In the latter case, a contrast between the New World and the outlook to which the newcomers were accustomed was inevitable, and would prove in time destructive to an inherited complex of tradition. Such a complex would have a chance to survive only where, in smaller communities, immigrants with the same national background continued to live together. In most cases the very exacting attempt toward assimilation to a new milieu made it seem desirable to forget whatever belonged to an older world. Later on, a new—generally the third—generation would turn their attention eagerly toward anything reminiscent of the old country—after they had attained a secure position in American life.

Of the attitude of the immigrants there is ample evidence. Particularly illuminating is the account given by a collector of folklore, himself of Greek descent, who recorded oral traditions among Greek immigrants in Boston in 1935. He wanted to find out, he says, to what extent this tradition had a meaning to these people, and he notes the difference in attitude of the men and the women. The men were reserved, saying that such things they had left behind with their village life and their herding of sheep. In America there were plenty of other things to worry about, and they refrained from talking about such things of the past, lest the children should hear them. "They were Americans and should be brought up in American affairs and not in the local affairs of a backward village." The attitude of the women was quite the opposite. They were pathetically eager to talk, and grateful that anybody would listen to their ancient wisdom. They were the guardians of tradition, and they felt lost when told by their husbands and children that these things were stupid. They were in possession of the necessary lore for every occasion, but in America such knowledge had no value. American ways they did not know and could not master, and how could they ever learn to do so, staying at home with the housework? And when the men advised them to put away their village lore, they offered them nothing to take its place. So when the collector came to them, they recaptured their old position of importance. For some hours they were glorified.

When the men mentioned the children and their aversion to letting them hear about the old days, they touched upon one of the main causes for the conscious avoidance of such "ancient things." The cause was what another writer has called "the destructive effects on the lives of millions of foreign born or first generation Americans of the prevalent belief that *difference* is something to be ashamed of, a belief that seems equally prevalent among children up to a certain age everywhere." This feeling of *not belonging* would naturally be immensely more marked in the entirely different environment where the immigrant found himself placed. Born in a mining town in Minnesota, one man who later became a state senator wrote, "It was not until I was a junior at the University that I realized that I was an American." The children were the chief means of contact for the immigrant women, and would pass on to them the constant criticism and suspicion of being foreign. A similar impression is vividly given in Carl Sandburg's autobiography, *Always the Young Strangers.* He grew up in a home where everything Swedish was derided, and the poor conditions from which the family had made good their escape were commented upon, while at the same time the rhythm of the daily life had preserved the native Swedish color. Swedish, however, was the language spoken in the Sandburg home. The father, who came to the States around 1870, could read but not write. Yet the autobiography of his son is not the story of a Swedish boy who gradually became an American; rather it gives the impression of a completely blank page, later filled with 100-per-cent American symbols.

Years have passed, and by now the attitude of the third generation seems completely altered, to judge from the vivid interest taken everywhere in the national past, in national costume dancing, etc., as also in the conscious effort of folklorists to retrieve what may have survived. Yet sometimes, in reading the account given by present-day writers, one has a strange feeling that the real background has been forgotten. A striking instance is found in an interesting book, *Wisconsin My Home,* written by a lady whose grandparents came from Norway. She mentions the belief, firmly held by her grandmother, in fairies and their child-stealing propensities, but she is of the opinion that these *Haugetusse*—the right term is used—were only gypsies who had the repute of stealing children. The force once held by the fairy belief is, as a matter of course, entirely foreign to the writer.

Evidence of a similar kind is to be found in most of the sources available, illustrating the point of view general among immigrants of recent periods. The intense pressure of a new community which had already developed a distinct American pattern of life and the immigrants' struggle to obtain a foothold in it, if not for themselves, then at least for their children, resulted in a conscious avoidance of traditional ideas and conceptions as of everything connected with their home country. For this reason traces of Scandinavian folklore are practically nonexistent. In the very extensive collection of folklore from a county in Illinois, with hundreds of items recorded, hardly a single one is to be found which may with confidence be ascribed to a Scandinavian source. A small verse of two lines in Danish is obviously copied from a modern Christmas card.

Apart from special cases of a group of immigrants from the same country living together, isolated from their surroundings by having a totally different language, such as Finnish or Lithuanian, modern immigrants seem to have brought very few contributions to the complex of American folklore. Accordingly, the European heritage, as far as folklore is concerned, is largely independent of these later arrivals; it was carried to various parts of America by early settlers from relatively few countries of western Europe. In this way European folklore in the Americas consists of elements from a rather small number of nationalities. To a European folklorist, therefore, American folklore does not appear as a multicolored web of strands, each with its own national color, but as a composition with characteristic features, each of them predominant in a definite part of the country. These main elements are English-Scotch, Irish, French, Spanish, and to a certain extent Dutch-German.

The folklore tradition carried by the early settlers was richer and more firmly rooted in their minds, simply because it belonged to an earlier period. Besides, in the new country to which they came, it did not have to accommodate itself to any new, already fixed pattern, since the traditions of the Indians were emotionally as well as linguistically too far removed from their own, and any extensive mutual influence was out of the question. A fact to a certain extent overlooked by European students is that the traditions of the early settlers are still accessible in some districts, where thirty or forty years ago the American way of life had not penetrated. Much to his surprise, the European folklorist will discover in certain localities reservoirs of European folklore of an earlier period.

Some few of such cases may be mentioned, as for example the reaction of Cecil Sharp on his visit to the southern Appalachians in 1916:

... I found myself for the first time in my life in a community in which singing was as common and almost as universal a practice as speaking. With us, of course, singing is an entertainment, something done by others for our delectation, the cult and close preserve of a professional caste of specialists. The fact had been forgotten that singing is the one form of an artistic expression that can be practised without any preliminary study or special training. ...

In 1910 Ray Mackenzie made similar observations in Nova Scotia, where the singing of traditional ballads still was alive but practiced only by the older generation, men seventy or eighty years old, and "any person of a younger generation who had acquired ballads traditionally had done so because of some unusual condition of character or of circumstance." From the South there is similar evidence. Ballads were sung about 1850. "Men knew nothing of books where the riches of balladry were treasured. To a Southerner the spoken word was weightier than the written." The "climate for balladry" was better than in the democratic states of New England in a society which a traveler in the year 1808 described in this way:

"The gentlemen pass their time in the pursuit of three things: all make love, most play and a few make money. With religion they have nothing to do, having formed a treaty with her, the principal article of which is: 'Trouble not us, nor will we trouble you.'" The references made have mostly been to the ballads, but one may safely conclude that other kinds of folk tradition as well have flourished in the same climate. Similar observations may be made about other districts; in the Ozarks, for example, eminent collectors such as Randolph and Raeburn have recorded and published a rich store of folklore. From their descriptions a picture emerges of an astonishingly old-fashioned community, persisting down almost to our own day. To quote Vance Randolph:

There are men in the Ozarks today who still hunt with muzzleloaded rifles, there are women who still use spinning wheels and weave cloth on homemade looms, there are minstrels who sing old English ballads brought over by seventeenth-century colonists, there are old settlers who believe firmly in witchcraft and all sorts of superstitions, there are people who speak an Elizabethan dialect that is well nigh unintelligible to the ordinary tourist from Chicago and points east. The typical Ozark native differs so widely from the average urban American that when the latter visits the hill country he feels himself among an alien people. The hillman recognizes the difference and refers to all outsiders as "furrinners" whether they come from North Dakota or South Germany.

The "reactions of an urban American," even if by no means typical, may be illustrated by some notes written by H. L. Mencken: "Such shabby and fleabitten villages I had never seen before, and such dreadful people. The villages were so barbaric that they did not even have regular streets. The houses such as they were were plunged down at every angle.—There were few fences; when one appeared it was far gone in decay." And a movie actor used still stronger words: "It is incredible that we have here in America people living in a lower state of culture than the savages we dispossessed." This is one point of view held by strangers without any sense of historical perspective. Another point, which concerns those who have a

sympathy with old folkways, is this, as expressed by Vance
Randolph:

It is only in such isolated places that we find the traditional American
nowadays, neither refined nor corrupted by the influence of European or
Asiatic civilization. There are not many real Americans left now, and
we do not understand him any more.... In a sense it is true that the
American people are making their last stand in the wilderness, and it is
here, if anywhere, that we must go to meet our contemporary ancestors
in the flesh.

As a stronghold of ancient tradition the Ozark region is
by no means unique, and a European folklorist will, much to
his surprise, discover other equally conservative districts such
as those isolated in the Kentucky mountains, where the
assimilation of modern conditions has set in only during the
last thirty or forty years. The way of living and the general
ideas of the older people of these valleys come vividly to light
in the writings of Marie Campbell, Jean Ritchie, and L. W.
Roberts, wherein also is made accessible a rich store of songs
and stories current among the inhabitants. The greater part
were of Scotch-Irish descent, but some were English, while
according to the estimate of one of the writers mentioned,
about 15 per cent had German ancestors. Occasionally there
were also peoples of other nationalities.

As might be expected, such backgrounds are easily detected
in the traditional stories current. Scotch-Irish matter predomi-
nates not only because there are so many descendants from
Scotch-Irish immigrants, but also because ancient traditions
have always been far better preserved in Ireland and the
Scottish Highlands than in other countries such as England.
This will explain why the Irish and Scotch immigrants brought
with them a far richer tradition than the others. "The tradition then," to quote Marie Campbell, "lived on for generations, unwritten except in the memories of the mountain
people for whom it formed a part of their daily life." Also in
the East, in the neighborhood of the great cities, districts are

found where for a long time the life and ideas of the inhabitants were equally isolated and conservative. Emelyn Gardner has, in a very interesting study, given an account of remote valleys of the Schoharie hills of New York, where, to use her own words written in 1937, "As I travelled by stagecoach from the prosperous farms and villages of the Schoharie valleys into the hills, where log houses, abandoned gristmills, and long covered bridges still lingered, I realized that I was passing from twentieth-century conditions into those of an earlier period." The ancestors of the people living here were of various nationalities, most of them perhaps German and Dutch, some English, and their descendants had faithfully followed their ways. They would refer to Pennsylvania, only some fifty miles away, as "furrin parts," and to the Atlantic Ocean as the "Great River" which it would take a body many days to cross. They were suspicious of strangers and "had no place for somebody they did not know nothing about."

Not too far away from these hills, in the piney country of New Jersey, Herbert Halpert found similar conditions and succeeded in recording a large amount of folklore during repeated visits after 1936. He also found the people extremely reserved and apparently suspicious of strangers, to them represented by tourists from the neighboring big cities, who loudly wondered how the people in this area could live without the conveniences and advantages of the city, and who laughed at the rural people's old-fashioned ways and beliefs and practical dress. And what was still worse, there had been published a sociological investigation of certain families in the piney country which in time made the whole district the target for newspaper feature writers eager to play up the general backwardness of the area. Like other isolated regions, the piney district was rapidly losing its older culture in the process of modernization.

To these instances many of the same kind could be added. The gradual advance of modernization and assimilation might be paralleled in any European country; it is equally well known in Scandinavia and other areas.

One may, however, doubt if such contrasts between ancient and modern ways of living were anywhere else as sharp as in America, especially in the parts of the country where British tradition was the dominating element and furnished the pattern. French tradition in Canada and elsewhere, like Spanish tradition in the South and West, seems to have lived on in communities that, to a larger extent, preserved the same characteristics as the country from which the immigrants came. In the East and North, however, there was a far larger admixture of other nationalities, and a more rapid development toward an urban American civilization. There only isolated, smaller groups of people were able to preserve their traditional heritage almost down to the present time, when naturally the contrast between their way of life and that of the cities had become more evident and striking.

To folklore and folklore studies the existence of these isolated reservoirs of tradition has opened up wide opportunities for collecting activities, and students of folklore have been offered the possibility of making a close examination of what happens in the transmission of song and story, especially if they are transmitted to entirely new surroundings. In many cases it is still possible, with a fair amount of confidence, to decide from which national groups of European tradition a ballad or story was derived, occasionally even to point to definite sources, such as the *Household Tales* of the Grimms. Such conclusions are important because they give the student a point of departure for examining the changes that followed upon the transmission of the well-known tales to a new and foreign world. Were there any definite tendencies to be observed? How far did the pattern and the setting adapt themselves to a new world?

One of the tales most widely disseminated, with a venerable pedigree, is "The Dragon Slayer." A variant was recorded in the Schoharie hills. The hero, a lazy peasant boy asleep by the roadside, is presented by an old woman with a sword guaranteed to cut off the heads of giants and an ointment that makes people sitting down stick to the seat. The tale is closely related to Scottish Highland versions, and the old lady who told it was of Scottish stock. The existence of giants and of such a magic sword and ointment is accepted, but the main incident of the tale, the saving of the king's daughter from the dragon, is somehow slurred over. The old woman told the boy that to get the king's daughter he would have to fight someone who wanted her for himself. When the boy located this someone, they fought for four days on the shore of a lake—invariably the scene for the dragon-fight—and the young man was the winner, probably (it is not expressly stated) because the princess had previously given him half an apple and a ring, the latter of which he had tied into his hair. With the ring in his hair, he came out atop. When asked who his anonymous antagonist was, the old lady replied in a whisper, "Why, the Old Un," and added, "The Devil is the last of the giants, you know." When asked about further details, she seemed puzzled and said: "I don't know anything about it except that my mother told the story that way," but she repeated the story word for word when the recording lady took it down again about a year afterward.

The same lady had another tale of the Bluebeard type, well told and fairly complete, with a characteristic opening incident showing that in this case also the tale had a Scottish pedigree. How such a story may disintegrate, when passing to a new audience, can be seen by comparing a variant of the same story from a white storyteller in North Carolina who said: "Lor, my granddaddy told me that story. I have not thought of it for thirty years." The story has dwindled down to a mere enumeration of the incidents, without even the slightest trace of any artistic consciousness or desire to tell a good story well. Note the ending, for example:

The girl has just found her sisters dead in the forbidden room. She is excited, drops her keys and gets them bloody. So he comes back and calls for his keys. She kept them hidden from him for several days as she did not want him to see them. At last she brought them and showed them to him. He told her to say a prayer. She prayed seven times and her seven brothers came just as he was going to kill her. And he ran away into the woods and has never been seen since.

Of greater interest are cases where one of the time-honored international tales has been exposed to the definite influence of some new element. One instance is concerned with the widely known story of "The Hidden Life," which is represented by a Texas version told in Spanish, "Cuerpo Sin Alma," in "Publications of the Texas Folklore Society," XIV (1938), 241-50. It was told by a student who had heard his grandmother tell it. Two other versions of the tale are briefly referred to by A. L. Campa. The story corresponds closely to the usual European versions, except for the opening incidents, where the Spanish story borrowed an incident best known from the apocryphal Book of Tobit: the evil spirit Asmodai carrying off the young brides on the night of their wedding. In this case the most enterprising of the deserted grooms goes to find the ogre and kill it. It is a well-told story, and the groom, like his many European counterparts, wins the gratitude of three animals by dividing a dead animal among them, thus being endowed with the power to take their shapes at will. The two Mexican versions briefly referred to by Mr. Campa are closely related, except in so far as they have chosen for an introduction another folktale cliché: the hero befriends a coyote and is directed to a lake where the bird-maidens are swimming, seizes the plumage of one of them, etc.

In an earlier volume of the "Publications" (XII [1935], 122-34), E. W. de Huff wrote a very interesting paper on the metamorphosis of the same tale (Type 302), which had been altered to "conform to the apperceptive basis of the Indians." In this case the father is cutting down trees, and is suddenly confronted by a giant lizard who claims his daughter. The tone of the story and the particulars of the setting have been altered, so that we have an instance of what happens when such ubiquitous stories are adopted into a new environment.

Ballads, being the most spectacular kind of folklore as well as the best preserved in tradition, immediately attracted the almost exclusive attention of students, and in the astonishing amount of ballad material brought together in the United States and in Canada, folklorists found rich and varied opportunities for studies of many kinds. The main approach was first from the standpoint of literature, especially the relationship between ballads and poetry in general on the lines followed in Professor Gummere's well-known book, *The Beginnings of Poetry* (1901). Accordingly, such studies were primarily, if not exclusively, concerned with ballads taken down from oral tradition, variants derived from written or printed sources being considered less important. A community was envisaged as evolving the ballads, the result of such creative action being later refined and further developed through transmission from one singer to another; in the end the contribution of the various carriers of tradition was summed up. As the conception of folklore widened, however, the ballads came to be considered not as an end in themselves but rather as tools, or as a means of getting in touch with the ancient, inherited conceptions and ways of living in a community dominated in the main by tradition—or, one might say, as a means of looking at the ballads not only, or mainly, from an aesthetic point of view, but from a geographical point of view. Printed versions and broadsides played equally important parts in the preservation and dissemination of ballads, and have continued to do so, because literacy was not limited to the educated classes. To quote B. A. Botkin: "The transference of oral tradition to writing and print does not destroy its validity as folklore, but rather, while fixing its form, helps to keep it alive, and diffuse it among those to whom it is not native or fundamental."

Printed versions, however, exert a certain influence upon tradition, as being by general agreement considered more authentic than what is not in print.

Such interplay between print and oral tradition is of special importance in a study of American ballads, but the question concerns not only these, but ballad studies everywhere. One has only to look at the commentaries added to the Danish ballads in Grundtvig's monumental edition to realize the part ancient broadsides played in their development. In his paper on "The Textual Transmission of Folklore" Professor Richmond has written an interesting study of some aspects of the problem. He notes that there is often a difference between various strains, one following oral tradition, another depending on print. He mentions as an instance the James Harris ballad, "The Demon Lover" (Child 243), first printed in Sir Walter Scott's *Minstrelsy*. In America, three variant strains can be distinguished, one derived from ancient oral tradition (Scottish), one from the broadsides, some of which are still preserved, and a third which represents a combination of these two.

Change, one may say, is one of the principal characteristics of folklore matter. Change may produce "better," more coherent or artistic results, but also may lead to disintegration and corruption of texts resulting from such difficulties as faulty memory or lack of power to interpret words and passages. A possible "improvement" would by later students probably only be considered possible in oral transmission, while the many improvements made by earlier editors such as Bishop Percy will be looked upon with distrust and disapproval. In American ballads, Professor Richmond has noted quite a number of changes due to the misunderstanding of a word or phrase. The most amusing is perhaps this one in the traditional ending to the ballad of two lovers united in death, such as were Barbara Allen and Sweet William. The original version has it:

> They buried the one in the old churchyard
> The other in the choir.

The choir as a burying place being unknown and the word
unfamiliar, the last line was changed in this way:

> They buried the one in the old churchyard
> The other in Ohio.

Such alterations may affect the tone of a ballad, but the
story itself may still remain unmodified. Other changes have a
deeper influence in altering the plot, and still deeper influence
in transposing the whole tone into another key. Of this type
is the general omission from American ballads of elements that
have their explanation in a belief in supernatural beings and
forces. The tendency was also found to be active in American
renderings of international folktales. Its function in balladry
is thus stated by Tristram Coffin:

Rationalization is one of the most powerful of all forces that work on the
ballad in Britain and in America, and as belief in ghosts, fairies and
other spiritual characters dwindles, everyday substitutes are provided,
so that an Elfin knight becomes a gypsy lover, and later an illicit lover,
or even a lodger, while a mermaid is replaced by a mortal mysterious
sweetheart. So strong is such rationalization that most of our modern
versions of ghost, witch, etc., ballads have lost all, or nearly all, traces
of the supernatural.

While this can be said of current American ballads of
European origin, it is even more directly applicable to native
American balladry. M. H. Laws has summed up the matter
thus: "Native American balladry, which is the product of a
more enlightened age than the old English balladry, contains
few fantastic or suggestive elements. No particular effort is
required to believe the central events."

This rationalization of elements presupposing a belief, or
a shadow of a belief, in unseen beings or forces is even more
apparent in the case of legends (tales that people believe to
record actual events) than in folktales and ballads. The forma-

tion of such legends is probably going on in every type of community, constituting an oral history, and being originally connected with something real, whether a certain place, person, or event. Oral history, however, differs from history proper because it has grown up under conditions inherent in oral tradition, involving constant alteration and being remodeled upon traditional patterns in passing from one storyteller to another. In European folklore it is the type of narrative that has survived the most changes, and still appears in kindred local legends which are equally well represented in most parts of the New World.

A special characteristic of these legendary tales is that they are rarely retold in an objective, disinterested way. In most cases a distinct tendency of some sort appears, and the explanation probably is that such tales had a function of another kind than that of the fictional folktales and ballads. They were meant to explain something, not to entertain and not primarily to relate actual facts. Furthermore, the explanation would, in most cases—at least in such stories of an earlier period—contain a reference, if perhaps only as a passing allusion, to extrahuman forces, to beings of another kind than man: beings closely related to humanity but still belonging to another order of things, a different world, one constantly interfering with our own and those who belong to it. A belief in this other world seems to be almost universal, though it has different forms and names in various countries. The inhabitants of the other world are generally called fairies, even if this term invariably seems to raise certain literary associations.

A European folklorist accustomed to meeting such conceptions almost at every corner in his own country is struck by their almost complete absence from American folklore, an absence in any event from places in American tradition where the general assimilation of all the various elements has proceeded for some time. In isolated communities, structurally and linguistically unchanged, such stories have survived, and have been current down to fairly recent times. The tale collections of Marie Campbell, for example, indicate that stories imported by the original Scotch-Irish settlers got a new lease on life. The same can be said to be true in the French settlements in Canada, and Richard M. Dorson's tale collections from Michigan's Upper Peninsula indicate a similar situation. Among people of these districts, the older generation still held a belief in "lutins," a kind of domestic spirit especially afflicting horses, sometimes riding them at night and leaving them next morning quite worn out, with intricate knots in their manes that defied any attempt at combing. In many cases, the lutins also had their special favorite among the horses and fed the chosen one on oats stolen from the rest. Such stories are popular all over Europe, and any number of them have been taken down in the Scandinavian countries. According to Dorson an attempt was even made to catch a lutin, by some men who had detected his presence by a glimmering of light in a stable. The men dug a deep hole in a heap of manure outside and formed two rows on the way from the stable to the hole. They had ready a sack, and eventually succeeded in catching the lutin. They kept him in the sack overnight in spite of all his struggles to get free. But when they released him in the morning, he disappeared so quickly that nobody was able to see what he looked like. This happened many years ago; lately skepticism has crept in. When in 1946 Dorson asked an old man about the lutins, the man said: "Years ago the oldtimers used to have that to scare people. The lutins were supposed to be an animal that curls the horse's mane, so it could hardly be combed any more. I heard that forty years ago, and I used to believe all that stuff."

In more recently established communities where racial unity has disappeared, the belief in this kind of being seems to be completely extinct. There are, to the best of my knowledge, no American traces recorded of the rich store of Scandinavian tradition of this type. This is largely due to the conscious reaction of the first generation of immigrants against such matters. With the disappearance of the belief itself the legends also decay, but cases are known of such stories having attained such a definite pattern that, like the fictional stories, they are able to live on. Take for example the well-known story about how some people got rid of a changeling by a strange procedure (brewing in an eggshell) which provoked him to reveal his age and true nature. In a version of the story told by a thirteen-year-old colored girl in Nova Scotia the point is virtually lost: A woman had a baby, and it was always quiet and well-behaved. Suddenly it became unruly, crying continuously. The woman took some eggs, filled the shells with water, put them on the stove, and left the room. When she heard the baby fall silent, she went in to see what had happened, "and here was a fairy and he had the baby under the bed, and he was the fairy. So she beat him and beat him and the baby cried: 'Oh, missus let me go,' so she let him go, and he came back nevermore."

The girl who told the story was quite positive that somehow a fairy was involved, but whether she actually had some further ideas about fairies, or believed in them, seems dubious. In any event, it was the story itself that caught her attention and made her remember it, in spite of her somewhat confused way of retelling it. There is, of course, the possibility that she had read the tale in some book, but no particulars are given by the editor. Another fairy story, equally well known in European countries, and recorded in the Middle Ages, is the one about a woman called in to act as midwife to a fairy mother. A couple of versions were taken down in America, and in neither case is the term *fairy* used, even though the strangeness of the visitor—as of the whole scene—is stressed. One version was related by a man who had heard it from his mother, a native of Ireland. According to the son, the man who sought her assistance was a stranger to her, a tall dark man, who refused to enter her house. He did not utter a single

word as they went together to his home; he just warned her
not to touch any food during her stay, and when everything
was all right, he saw her home. No distinct trace of a "supernatural" background is preserved. The motifs of the stranger's
refusal to enter the midwife's house, and his later warning not
to touch the food in his own house, were part of the Irish
original, but in the rendering given they fit in equally well
with common experience and constitute a wholly human scene.

Something more nearly supernatural is preserved in an
Ozark story, even if the term *fairy* is not used. This story
obviously also had an Irish or West-Scotch background. It is
more elaborately told. The woman, often called in when children were born, heard "a noise like little feet coming in, but
she couldn't see nobody" until she felt a stream of cold water
in her eyes. Then she saw a little chap with a red cap on his
head and a feather stuck into it. "She knew at once who he was
the minute she laid eyes upon him but he told her not to be
afraid." The rest of the story follows the usual pattern, except
that the motif of the ointment used for the eye of the newly
born infant, and accidentally applied by herself to her own
eye, is altered into a kind of ceremony: a stream of water
necessary before a human being would be able to see fairies.
This again necessitated an alteration in the last episode of the
tale. In the standard version she sees the visitor later on,
much to his consternation, and he makes her blind in one eye;
but in the Ozark tale he exclaims, "My goodness! I was so
excited about my wife the other day that I forgot to fix things."
She again feels the stream in her eyes and loses her power to
see the fairies.

Folk belief is intimately related to legends, even legends
that may have attained a definite shape and thus entered the
cycle of tales told for entertainment and not involving the
acceptance of any particular belief. The background, an actual
belief in another race of beings, is sparsely represented in
American folklore, and, as it appears, is to be found alive only

where a close connection with the conceptions and ways of living of the first immigrants is occasionally recorded. Of more interest is the evidence of fairy belief still preserved among the older generations in the Kentucky mountains, where collectors have found people who report they have been exposed to fairy arrows or have seen fairies frolicking upon some near hillside.

Why, then, did such beings not survive the transfer? The question is by no means easy to answer. More recent immigrants may, in their desperate struggle to gain a secure foothold in a new society, have tended to aim at a total discarding of such elements. And in the isolated districts where settlers may have preserved ancient notions, these are now vanishing as the process of amalgamation to American city ways proceeds apace. It is less easy to account for abandonment of fairy belief by the original settlers, who most likely had shared the general attitude of other Europeans of their time toward notions of this type. Is the disappearance of such ideas to be explained by the fact that fairy belief had no function, no position in the new settlements? Perhaps there is in such belief an element deeply interwoven with a long, unbroken settlement, a kind of domestication, or close relationship, dependent upon special associations with a familiar scene. Of all this those first settlers had nothing, but were exclusively dependent upon their own resources and energy. Their attitude toward their surroundings, toward the untamed nature that constantly had to be conquered, prevented that sense of familiarity between persons and places that seems a necessary prelude to a belief in fairies. Some slight parallel may perhaps be found in those areas of the Scandinavian countries settled recently (within the last hundred years) by people coming from other parts. In remote valleys in northern Norway farmers from the south have taken possession and broken new ground. Among them no tradition of this kind has been developed, except as vague memories, more or less held in ridicule, of such stories as told by the original settlers from their home districts. Life has been too hard, the conditions for survival too exacting, and the result is a marked skepticism toward anything not pertaining to daily life and work.

Witches and ghosts, however, survived the transition very well, and both have, at least up to recent times, retained influence on the acts and conceptions of many older people. One has to remember that at the time the first settlers arrived, witchcraft was not a superstition but a dogma accepted by churches of every denomination, and furthermore a dogma of far greater importance to daily life than many other dogmas. As for ghosts, they have a remarkable ability to survive and interfere in almost every kind of mental climate. There is, for example, a very interesting essay on "The Characteristics of New York Ghosts," and ghostly hitchhikers make use of the latest model automobiles. Perhaps the reason for this survival is to be found in the intimate relationship between man and ghost, founded not on reasoning but on what one may call an instinctive protest by man against the inevitable separation of body and spirit. Ghosts inhabit a province very close to our own, and their existence is vouched for not only by popular religion but also by adherents of parapsychology and related advance groups of students, desperately intent upon extending the limits of human knowledge.

American folklore stories of witches and their doings are numerous, and their background—British, German, or Spanish —is as a rule apparent. Some stories that have acquired ⸱ definite epic pattern recur everywhere, such as the story abou⸱ the man who tried to follow a witch on her nightly expedition, but failed through a mistake in the formula to be used. Apart from such migratory stories, which emphasize the narrative rather than the "lesson," the belief in the existence of magic powers, the practices of "wise women," or men, is as familiar in many American districts as in European countries. The actual witch is probably everywhere part of the past, but her literal descendants are still active, and the mere suspicion that anybody is dealing in witchcraft may in several old-fashioned communities still raise adverse feelings, and persons suspected of such activities may still be ostracized by their neighbors. The *JAFL* editor of the 1880's was correct when he stated that superstitious beliefs still play an active part in the lives of many people in America; and his statement retains its validity today.

Even if this European folklore heritage will in due time be dissipated, this does not by any means imply the disappearance of folklore. In spite of the overpowering force of everything new, of all the matter for entertainment and for reflection and speculation which, through ever more accessible and powerful intermediaries, is spreading all over the world, the listeners still have their own contributions to make, their own stories to tell, their own beliefs to connect with modern happenings. Omens, in older days associated with, say, the strange behavior of birds, may also be taken from the lights of a cinema or from the license plates of cars. Persons in the limelight will still serve as centers for additional stories, made up or taken from many a venerable source and rearranged to fit a new hero. Striking instances may be found in the cycle of tales attached to such American heroes as Paul Bunyan or Johnny Appleseed, tales which come to adopt the characteristic features of myth, explaining the origin of mountains and rivers, and gradually swelling into a new type of genuinely native American folklore. In these tall stories the European heritage also survives; any reader of a collection of this type will find in a large percentage the same pattern used in European tales of a much earlier date. A European folklorist, without claiming any extensive knowledge of materials of this kind, will yet look at them with a sincere interest as evidence of the persistent vigor of folklore, a demonstration that it is not merely a thing of the past, seen from a point far away. The lesson will be that folklore, a complex formed by man not according to what is taught in schools or read in books, but developing from the fundamental trends in his mind, is still alive.

In this way, then, your European folklorist has found himself confronted with a new province, much more interesting and varied than he could ever have imagined. His feelings may be said to be akin to those of a visitor to one of your magnificent museums, with the difference that the exhibits are not objects and illustrations of human progress, but records, however intangible, of what man has imagined and believed in, of songs and tales and of strange legends and vanishing customs. Unknown artists have contributed to such expressions, generations have held such beliefs and followed traditional practice and felt themselves safeguarded. The European folklorist's most surprising experience would, however, be the discovery of the unity of all such things, a unity embracing the wide world, embracing points that would be understood by inhabitants of an out-of-the-way Scandinavian parish as well as by old-fashioned residents of East Texas or the Hill Country. And the discovery of this unity, the sense of its force, and the hope for its influence are perhaps the chief experience your European folklorist will carry with him on his return to his own familiar haunts.

Folklore in a Literate Society

MODY C. BOATRIGHT

THERE WILL, I predict, be readers, particularly among those who teach English composition to college freshmen and have made the frustrating discovery that Johnny can't read, who will maintain that this essay can have no reference to the United States. Yet that is the reference intended. For even though Johnny can't read as well as his teacher wishes, and even though Americans read fewer books than the British, the scripts they listen to have been written by somebody. Besides, nearly everybody reads something—if not the Philadelphia *Bulletin*, then the *Readers' Digest*, the *Wall Street Journal*, the Dell Comic books, or the Rexall Almanacs. But even if there is an American who reads nothing at all, he lives in a culture whose most important determinant is the written word.

What happens in America, therefore, has a significant bearing on what happens to folklore in a literate society.

When you read, let us say, Louis Adamic's description of a peasant wedding in Yugoslavia, with its mock fight for possession of the bride, suggestive of a remote antiquity when marriages were made by capture, you say, "How quaint. This is folklore." What do you say when you read about the weddings reported in the society pages of your local newspaper? Here are a couple of examples:

Given in marriage by her father, the bride wore a white crystal waltz length gown with inset eyelet crystalette panels and bouffant skirt. The shoulder length veil of illusion was held by pearlized orange blossoms. . . .

Following the ceremony, a reception was held in the fellowship hall of the church. After a trip to Florida, the couple will live in ——.

Given in marriage by her father, the bride wore a floor length dress of lace over taffeta designed with a basque bodice, brief sleeves and a tiered skirt. Her fingertip veil was attached to a cap of Chantilly lace re-embroidered with pearls and sequins.

[Honor attendants] wore waltz length dresses of seafoam green chiffon over taffeta and net with matching crown headpieces and carried baskets of majestic daisies and English ivy.

Are the American weddings any less folkish because the bride and her mother had the advice of Emily Post and Neiman-Marcus rather than, or in addition to, that of the village elders? At least the veil remains, though its antique function has long been forgotten.

Other questions arise. When a carpenter learns to frame a roof by serving an apprenticeship and receiving instruction by word of mouth from a man who has received his in the same way, you may call his art a folk craft, that is, a tradition that has been handed down orally. But suppose the carpenter has studied a book on roof framing? Or—what is often true these days—he has gone to school and can prove the Euclidean propositions upon which the craft is based?

I have read in collections of folklore descriptions of Czech beer parties in honor of a christening. But I have never found in what purported to be a collection of folklore a description of a publisher's cocktail party in honor of an author's latest book. Yet each follows a historically determined pattern; each is a custom of a group with a common body of tradition. This is not to say that the traditions are of equal duration, or that they have been transmitted in exactly the same way.

One effect of literacy is high specialization and another is nationalism. As a nation gets bigger, its people become increasingly divided into occupational and other groups. Folklore has been mainly concerned with certain of these groups, to the exclusion of others. It began in Europe as a study of "vulgar errors" or "popular antiquities," and even after Thom proposed the term *folklore* in 1846 its content for the most part continued to be the social anthropology of European peasants, and later of "primitive" people of other continents. Thus arose the concepts of survival and arrested development.

Thus arose too the idea that a "folk" must be a primitive group isolated from the contaminating influence of modern civilization. Mary Austin, for example, was able to find only three folk groups in the United States: the Red Indians, the Southern Negroes, and the Southern Mountaineers. These are all isolated geographically or socially or both. But there are other kinds of isolation, and there are many groups within the mass. An occupation, for example, unites its members, and at the same time partially separates them from the mass. Each occupation has its lore—partly belief, partly custom, partly skills —expressed in anecdotes, sagas, tales, and the like. Each individual in a literate society plays a multiplicity of roles, belonging as he does to more than one group. Take for example the railroad conductor who is also a baseball fan. He has a body of tradition appropriate to each role. He knows how to behave in each role, and he knows the verbal lore of each. He knows the witticisms that pass between conductors and passengers. He can tell you apocryphal tales about Jay Gould and Collis Huntington; he knows about Casey Jones and the slow train through Arkansas. He knows too about Casey at the bat, and has at his command all the formulas for heckling the other team and the umpire. Our culture is the richer for this pluralism.

Yet the mass in the United States may, I think, be properly referred to as a folk. For in spite of divisive influences of specialization, of geography, of race, the American people have more in common than in diversity. Charles Wilson and Walter Reuther are divided by class interest. Wilson believes that what is good for General Motors is good for the United States. Reuther believes that what is good for labor is good for the United States. One believes in the trickle-down theory of prosperity; the other in the seep-up theory of prosperity. But they both believe in prosperity. They speak the same language, have much the same concept of the mission and destiny of America, and neither is a conscious enemy of capitalism. One cannot assert that there is any one belief that every American accepts, but the presence of dissent does not prove the absence of a common body of tradition.

Even in a preliterate society tradition is never wholly static. One consequence of literacy is an acceleration of change. Learning develops not only new techniques but new values as well. As long as the American Negro saw no prospect of sharing in the white man's rising standard of living, his folklore concerned the values available to him. Charms took the place of the medical service he could not afford; superstition took the place of the education that was denied him. He consoled himself with tales covertly satirical of the white man and with the hope of justice when he crossed the River Jordan and was gathered to Abraham's bosom. Once convinced of the possibility of sharing in the good things about him, however, he announces without regret that Uncle Tom is dead—but not Uncle Tom's music, which he will cite with justifiable pride as a major contribution to American culture. This shift in emphasis is illustrative of one change folklore undergoes in a literate society.

Another change involves the crafts. The first effect of the industrial revolution is to drive out the folk crafts. Blankets from New England mills take the place of homemade quilts. Brussels and Axminster carpets appear on floors once covered by hooked rugs and rag carpets. Furniture comes from Grand Rapids rather than from the shop of the local cabinetmaker. In time, however, certain countervailing influences assert themselves. There is a revolt against the monotony of both the mass-produced article and the routine job by which most Americans earn their living; and as the shorter work week, the expansion of the service industries, and the availability of household appliances create leisure, and often boredom, people take up hobbies, and hobbies germinate new industries serving them.

Markets are found for textile mill-ends, and the Rose of Sharon and the Wedding Ring begin to appear on beds; department stores display yarn and burlap, and hooked rugs reappear. The makers of power tools put on do-it-yourself campaigns, and men begin turning out coffee tables and four-posters in their basements. Most of the craftsmen will work from patterns furnished by their suppliers or the hobby magazine, but a few will create their own designs.

New crafts appear. Teen-aged boys learn that by doing certain things to their motors they can increase the noise, if not the power, of their jalopies. When this activity spreads over the country, somebody realizes that here is a clientele for a new magazine and *Hot Rod* appears on the newsstands. Then machine shops begin making the parts and selling kits to noncraftsmen, who, if they can afford to, may have their mechanics instal them.

Even so, for the first time since the Stone Age great masses of people have opportunity to give play to the instinct of workmanship, to find relief from the monotony of their jobs, and in some degree to express whatever individuality they are endowed with.

As has been suggested by reference to the wedding veil, not all old customs perish. In a culture dedicated as ours is to a continuously rising standard of material well-being, a custom is likely to survive, though with a changed significance, if its observance increases the sales of goods and services. Readers of Keats know that at one time a girl could, by performing certain rites on the Eve of St. Agnes, see a vision of her future husband. The rites are no longer performed. They required no purchasable equipment. Not so with the suitable observance of Christmas, Thanksgiving, Easter—and now Halloween, for of late we bribe the tricksters with store-bought candy. We invent Mother's Day and Father's Day, spacing them carefully so they will not come too close to other already established occasions for spending money.

The pageantry that used to be associated with other occasions—the tournament for example—will be adapted to the publicizing of local products. The Queen of Love and Beauty becomes the Queen of Goats:

FREDERICKSBURG [Texas], July 25 (CTS)—A beautiful queen, as much at home in ranching jeans as in regal robes that denote her reign over the Mohair Realm, will officiate at the 38th annual coronation, show and sale of the Texas Angora Goat Raisers' Association here Aug. 1, 2, and 3.

Her Mohair Majesty, we learn, will have the title of "Angora Queen of the Universe," will be attended by "a score of attractive duchesses," and will receive the homage of the queen of the South Texas Fairs and Fat Stock Shows, the queen of the Gillespie County Fair, and the Farm Bureau queen.

In a literate society verbal folklore will be disseminated not only by loggers, cotton pickers, oil field workers, and traveling salesmen, but also by historians, biographers, fictionists, and journalists, not to say folklorists. Songs, tales, proverbs will be published and read and some of them put into a wider oral circulation. In this process narrative lore, in particular, will undergo change. In the 1920's the journalists discover Paul Bunyan, who by this time is not only a logger but also an oil field worker, and begin writing about him for the general magazines. In order to make their material go as far as possible, they invent some tales and rewrite others long in the oral tradition, including many that have no connection with either logging or oil field work. In the meantime the loggers and oil field workers have become skilled manipulators of machines—power saws, power loaders, tractors, rotary rigs, and the like—and have lost interest in Bunyan. He becomes a national rather than a local or occupational folk character, standing for little more than bigness and strength. As Richard Dorson has observed, the journalists take him from the folk and give him back to a larger folk, but with a changed character and significance. And this will be true of any hero who attains more than local fame. Without the aid of writers he cannot move out of the province in which he has been created. The writers in moving him out must remold him into a type intelligible to the larger audience. Thus bad men become Robin Hoods, cowboys become knights-errant, backwoods politicians become symbols of militant democracy, lowly animals become symbols of lowly folk. Incidents are reported and transferred from one region to another. The journalists who covered the first oil boom, for example, garnered a considerable sheaf of rags-to-riches stories. Later journalists reported the same stories from other fields, and often in good faith, for the stories appear sometimes to have come from Pennsylvania to Texas first by word of mouth.

This essay will have achieved its purpose if it has raised more questions than it has answered. It has been written on the assumption that the processes which create folklore do not cease when a society becomes literate, and that the folklore of any culture will reflect the values of that culture. If it has demonstrated anything, it is that the oral and written traditions are not most fruitfully conceived as separate and distinct. Each is continually borrowing from the other as the processes of adaptation and creation continue.

Twister Tales

HOWARD C. KEY

LAST FALL when I offered to read a paper in Dallas at the 1957 meeting of the Texas Folklore Society, I knew that April 12 was right in the middle of the tornado season. But, believe me, I did not know that one of the most spectacular and devastating storms in Texas history was to precede me on the program.* I had not planned to have my words illustrated in such tragic fashion nor my small thunder so effectively stolen. Petty thievery such as this, however, is minor compared to some of the grim jokes that twisters like to play.

The tornado gets its name from the Spanish *tornar,* meaning "to turn" or "to twist." The nickname *twister* is the most popular and logical English equivalent. Most people used to refer to this dreaded storm as a cyclone, and many still call it that. A cyclone, however, is just a large, unspectacular area of low pressure no more like a tornado than an elephant is like a flea.

The tornado is not only the smallest but the most violent, power-packed, and concentrated storm known to man, with winds in excess of 400 miles per hour and an explosive force not yet measured. Its path ranges in width from a few yards to two miles. And the destruction caused in this narrow area is far more complete than that wrought by a hurricane or any other atmospheric disturbance over a wider area.

There is no point in my describing the appearance of tornadoes after their TV debut in Dallas ten days ago. The funnel

*Toll of the Dallas tornado on April 2, 1957, was 10 dead and 183 injured; property damage came to $4,000,000. Alert television cameramen tracked the twister step-by-step.

shape by which tornadoes are known showed up rather well in this performance. But the funnel configuration is by no means inevitable. Sometimes the cloud is thin and ropelike, with curves and convolutions. Sometimes it is wide and squat, and sometimes it is present but practically invisible or transparent.

The exact cause of tornadoes has never yet been determined, although the circumstances surrounding their birth are now pretty well known. They are always associated with thunderstorms, but the electrical activity may be so far away or so high in the air as to go unnoticed at the exact time of the tornado. Thunderstorms can be predicted. The only trouble has been to locate those in which tornadoes may form.

Tornadoes can occur at any time of the day or night, during any month of the year, and at any place in the world. But they like best the late afternoon or early evening of the spring months (February through June) in the middle western and southwestern part of the United States. Occasionally a vagrant member of the family will wander into New England or the Pacific Northwest, and lately there have been many impressive forays into the Great Lakes region and the Deep South. The real homeland, though, is the vast plains of the West-Southwest, the area between the Rocky Mountains and the Mississippi.

In this area, particularly during the spring, a situation conducive to violent weather regularly exists. Warm, moist air flowing up from the Gulf of Mexico meets cool, dry air coming in from the Rocky Mountains region or Canada. This meeting point is what we call a front. The cool air runs under the warm air, forcing it upward or crowding it together so that it has to rise. It is in these moist, warm areas of rising air ahead of a cold front that tornadoes are most likely to form.

Once started, they seem to keep forming or re-forming ahead of the cold air as it moves across the country from west to east. In many instances the actual path of destruction will be not only narrow but short. The length of a tornado trail

would probably average between 10 and 15 miles. But there
have been storms that moved across three states. The longest
on record is a storm on May 26, 1917, that started about noon
at the Mississippi River a few miles below Hannibal, Missouri,
and finally wound up at 7:30 P.M. near the Ohio line in southeastern Indiana, leaving a continuous path of destruction 293
miles long and from one-quarter to three-quarters of a mile
wide. The most fearful and destructive tornado on record
started in south central Missouri on March 18, 1925, at exactly
1:00 P.M. Without once lifting or abating, it moved cross country to southwestern Indiana, a distance of 219 miles, in three
hours and eighteen minutes, at an average forward speed of
more than sixty miles per hour. This tornado struck several
sizable towns, killed 689 people, badly injured 2,000 others,
and destroyed property valued at $17,000,000.

The most deadly single strike ever made by a tornado
occurred May 9, 1840, at Natchez, Mississippi, where 317
people were killed outright and an undetermined number died
later of injuries. An interesting phenomenon of this storm was
that in certain sections of its path the leaves and buds were
not stripped off growing plants as usual but were seared and
crisped as if by fire. Vast areas of plant growth blackened and
died within a few days after the storm. A tornado in St. Louis
in 1896 traveled the entire breadth of the city from west to east
and killed 306 people. In its journey it blew fine straw through
plate glass without breaking the glass, and drove a two-by-four
pine scantling through one of the steel girders on the Eads
bridge.

The two most deadly tornadoes ever to visit Texas were at
Waco on May 11, 1953, and at Goliad on May 18, 1902. Each
storm killed 114 people and injured hundreds of others. The
Rock Springs tornado in 1927 killed 74, while 70 died in a
storm at Sherman in 1896.

But statistics do not tell the true story of tornadoes—because
tornadoes are pretty much like people. They are born, they

have their careers, they die and go to heaven. They have their likes and dislikes, their whims and ambitions; they have their various appetites, their impulses good and bad. They are all individuals.

In order to find out the whole truth about tornadoes you have to go to a friend of a friend of a friend who has been in one or seen one or come upon the remains of one. Like battle-scarred veterans, those who have actually experienced such storms often can't talk coherently or don't want to talk. Folk-lorists and myth-searchers know better than anyone else that you have to get a good distance away from something before you can find out the truth about it.

My psychoanalysis of the tornado personality is therefore based chiefly on off-the-spot, antiscientific oral investigation. I have come to only one conclusion. Tornadoes are like women. No matter what you say about them, they will make a liar out of you.

For example, the first trait on my list happens to be the one tragically refuted by the Dallas storm ten days ago. My earlier research had indicated that tornadoes seem well disposed toward children, especially infants. You know, of course, that many of the victims of this recent storm were small children. Nevertheless, out of more than three hundred tales in my collection, thirty-two deal with miraculous preservation of infants and twelve are essentially the same story in different settings. Many a tornado has mauled the rest of the family and blown a house away and left baby cooing in his crib, or set him down gently in some safe spot.

One tornado skipping through southeastern Kansas about fifty years ago scooped a six-weeks-old infant out of its cradle and deposited him unscathed, though plastered with mud, in the middle of a haystack a mile away. The haystack was several hundred yards distant from the actual path of the tornado, and seemed not to have a single straw disarranged except those landed on by the baby. An old hound dog made the discovery a few hours later and notified his master by curious tail waggings, whining, and other signs. The baby, Bill Suddath, is alive and well today as described by his cousin Tom Suddath, who told me this story in Phoenix, Arizona, in 1929. Tom owns a descendant of the dog.

Another tornado picked a baby out of its crib and dropped him face up in a puddle of water a few blocks away. The water came just to the baby's ears, and he was apparently enjoying his bath when found by rescuers. This story came to me recently from a student whose home is near White Deer in the Panhandle. It parallels rather closely three other accounts of miraculous preservations, also from West Texas. This is the only place in the United States, apparently, where there isn't enough water to drown babies.

Tornadoes are partial to infants, but they seem not to bear particular malice to children either. It has been the practice of rural school boards of the Southwest and Middle West to locate their beacons of learning on the highest, most exposed ground available. As a consequence, tornadoes are always bungling into schoolhouses full of children. But the death toll in these mishaps has been astonishingly low. One storm struck and totally demolished a rural school in Kansas with eighty-five pupils in it. Only two children were killed. This same storm struck another schoolhouse with sixteen children, gave all of them a free ride for several hundred yards, and set them down unharmed, but badly injured the teacher.

An eyewitness described to me a tornado near Frankston, Texas, in the late 1920's. The storm came up about three o'clock of a sultry afternoon in late April. My informant, teacher and principal, was conducting a class in geography in a four-room, four-teacher school with a total of seventy-eight students. All at once one of the children pointed out the window and yelled, "Look at the fire!" The teacher went to the window and saw what appeared to be a huge column of smoke rising about a mile and a half away to the southwest. She recalls very clearly a red glow inside or around the column that gave it every appearance of a bonfire. Presently, however, flying debris and a visible whirling motion made her realize that the column of smoke was really a tornado. With a calmness that she disclaims having felt, she ordered the children to return at once to their seats and begin studying. They did so. (This was in the good old days when children were accustomed to obeying teachers.)

Meanwhile she ran to each of the other rooms and warned the other teachers. They decided in a hurried conference to take shelter in a ravine about half a block northwest of the schoolhouse, just below the boys' playground. She remembers announcing to her class that a storm was coming and that they would go to the creek right away—"but no pushing or shoving, please. There will be plenty of time."

The children were very orderly while getting out of the classroom; but once on the outside, even the youngest could see that there wasn't so much time as she had said. The storm was roaring frightfully, and all could now see trees and boards and debris flying through the air only a short distance away. My informant said that the horrible thought flashed through her mind accusingly, "I have waited too long and taken too much time warning the others. I should have let the kids go when I first saw the cloud." All of them broke into a wild dash for the ravine. The teachers (two of them rather elderly ladies) followed as fast as they could.

Actually the storm was not so close as they had thought. There must have been about two minutes' time after the last teacher had clambered down beneath the six-foot embankment before the storm hit. At the very end of this brief interval, Miss Annie, third- and fourth-grade teacher, gave a scream scarcely audible in the roar of the tornado. "Oh, my God, Maxine and Patsy!" Two little girls from her room had been excused and were presumably in the girls' toilet on the other side of the schoolhouse several hundred yards away.

It was too late. The tornado was already arriving. The

schoolhouse seemed to shudder before their eyes; and then, to
the delight of most of the onlookers, it just went all to pieces.
The air was dark; branches and lumber were flying everywhere.

It was over before they knew what had happened. Not a
child was touched or even scratched, including the two little
girls who had fled up the road toward home when they
emerged from the little girls' room and saw the tornado almost
upon them. Each of the four teachers received painful injuries,
one a broken leg, another bruises and lacerations; my informant
suffered a rather deep cut over the right shoulder blade.

Another one of the gentler aspects of the tornado's nature
is its regard for flowers, especially cut flowers in vases. On more
than one occasion when houses, walls, and furniture have been
ripped to shreds and scattered over many acres, a vase of roses
will be left undisturbed on a living room table. This story has
come to me, with little variation, from four states: Arkansas,
Oklahoma, Texas, and Louisiana. It is almost impossible not
to conclude that tornadoes love flowers.

But there are some things tornadoes do not care for at all.
Chickens, for example. It's hard to say why these storms pick
on chickens, but that's exactly what they do. One authority
claims that the air in the quills of chicken feathers explodes as
a result of the vacuum on the outside—and pop! off come the
feathers. Anyway, one well-authenticated tornado picked a
whole flock of thirty chickens absolutely clean and left them
sitting side by side on their perches in the chicken house, bolt
upright but dead. One storm wafted a Louisiana rooster several
miles, stripped him of feathered finery and set him down naked
in a yard full of strange hens—still full of vitality and vanity.
Another very violent and whimsical tornado is reported to have
blown a rooster into a jug, leaving only his head sticking out.

A tornado near Clyde, Texas, was even caught sucking eggs.
The family took shelter in a cellar where the mother kept a pan
of fresh eggs on a shelf near the entrance. My informant, a
person of undoubted integrity, reports that before the eyes of

all of them these eggs took off in a row, one at a time, and passed through a hole in the cellar door. The pan finally followed and clamped itself against the opening to stop the suction.

Tornadoes habitually mistreat other farm animals besides chickens. A story is told of a farmer who was in his barnyard feeding his mules when a tornado struck. The wind yanked up the farmer and his mule, and somewhere aloft set the farmer down on the mule's back. The pair landed right side up about half a mile away, but the mule hit the ground running and put another five miles between himself and home before the farmer could stop him. The tale is told, too, of a milkmaid left sitting on a stool while bossy and barn took off through the Kansas atmosphere.

I have talked to only one person who was actually lifted off his feet and transported by a tornado—Colonel William Porter. He tells a graphic story of a tornado that lashed Cisco, Texas, on April 18, 1893. When he and his wife were preparing to eat supper, they were disturbed by a few bursts of hail the size of baseballs. Shortly after this display stopped, they could hear an awful roar and crackling—"kinda like a big, big frying pan full of hot grease." They rushed out on the front porch and saw the tornado not far away. It looked just like a great dark green watermelon upended and dragging along the ground. He and Mrs. Porter watched it in fascination for several minutes before they realized it was coming toward them fast. They ran into the front room of their house just as the wind struck. Mr. Porter yelled to his wife to crawl under the bed.

About this time he found out that instead of running toward the back room, as he intended, he was waving his arms and legs somewhere in midair. Seconds later he slammed into some object that felt like a wire fence. Then he heard music and decided he was either dead or dying. It was their new player piano, the kind that had to be pumped with foot pedals. The suction of the storm had somehow started it going and it was appropriately playing "Nearer My God to Thee," a musical roll that happened to be in place when the storm struck.

Both Mr. Porter and the piano were lodged in the branches of a big pecan tree about fifty yards from his house and had to be helped down by neighbors, but neither was much damaged. This incident argues for a certain artistic quality in the tornado's nature.

Tornadoes like to let trains and automobiles know who is boss. One such storm waylaid an eastbound Northern Pacific freight train, uncoupled the locomotive from a string of cars, and set it down full steam ahead on a parallel track headed west. Exactly the same kind of thing happened to an automobile in another storm. It is reported that the driver, a California man, went thirty miles back over the Kansas plains before he found out he was headed in the wrong direction.

A tornado has been known to teach a Sunday School lesson. Primus and Frankie Jenkins, a Negro couple living close to the Trinity River bottom near Groveton, Texas, had an argument about a fishing trip one Sunday morning. Frankie maintained that the Lord didn't intend colored folks, or white folks either, to go fishing on Sunday. Primus said fishing was just fun and not work and the Lord wouldn't care. He left before time for church and went down to the river. Frankie stayed at home and attended church. About two o'clock in the afternoon the twister hit through the river bottom and continued onward near the Jenkins shanty. Primus was in a boat on the river when the vortex passed quite near him, sucking up water like a big fountain. In the commotion his boat turned over and dumped out a string of fish he had caught. At home Frankie was praying. "It was the onliest thing I knowed to do," she said. As soon as the storm had passed she went out on the front porch. A few steps away in the yard lay a big, fat 25-pound mud cat, flip-flopping around in the rain. Frankie and Primus ate catfish that night for supper, but Primus never again fished on Sunday.

Another tornado of moral rectitude visited the western part

of Haskell County, Texas, many years ago. A hard, rich farmer, a widower, owned a lot of land in those parts. Nearly everybody for five or six miles owed him money or rented from him. Several women were hoping to marry him, but he would not tumble. He saw a tornado coming in one evening and crawled under his feather bed. An errant finger of wind sought him out along with his mattress. The farmer was never able to say what had happened in the minute or so he was in the grasp of the storm, but he was found by the side of the road covered with feathers from head to foot, just as if he had been tarred and feathered. Doctor and nurses (one of them marriageable) spent more than two hours pulling feathers out of him. He recovered, married the nurse, and lived to be a much kinder man.

One of the most accommodating tornadoes on record streaked through a small farming community about 35 miles southwest of Ponca City, Oklahoma. The home of a neighbor of my informant was slightly damaged in this encounter. The windows were blown out and loose objects apparently rattled around at great rate, for the lady of the house received a bad cut on the thigh and a blow on the head which knocked her unconscious. She had that morning written a letter to her sister in Ponca City saying that she would come to town soon for a visit. This letter was lying stamped and addressed on the dining room table and disappeared during the storm. Yes, you guessed it. This letter fell uncancelled in Ponca City only a block away from its intended destination. Fifteen minutes later it was in the hands of the city sister. Thirty minutes later, a call from the hospital informed her that her correspondent was a patient there.

Further proof that twisters are sometimes disposed to be helpful is the story told by a farmer living near Austin, Texas. A tornado came through his back yard and uprooted a fine peach tree which he had nursed successfully through several dry years. Such an ill deed would have been highly exasperating to any Texas farmer. But in this case the big wind obligingly dropped an equally fine young pecan tree into the gaping hole left by the uprooted peach tree. When the farmer went out to survey the damage, he saw the pecan tree standing, or rather leaning, embarrassed, where the peach tree had been. He pushed his new plant to an upright position and tamped down the earth around it. The tree lived and is growing today. Each year it yields a fine crop of paper-shelled pecans—with a peach flavor. This special flavor has been vouched for by Mody Boatright, who lives in the neighborhood, and had the nuts first hand from the farmer himself.

A sprightly Alabama twister lifted the roof of one house, broke open a trunk in the attic, and scattered family photographs and heirlooms among relatives nearly fifty miles away.

Near Desdemona, Texas, a tornado blew in on the Jordan family just in time for supper. Hearing the roar, Papa, Mama, and the three kids scrambled up from the table, where they had just said grace, and lit out for the storm house. The vacuum inside the vortex exploded the house and demolished everything in it except the dining room table. This was left untouched. And they were able to finish their supper by the light of a coal oil lamp left burning in the center of it.

Although inclined to redistribute private property, tornadoes are not basically communistic. The following story was told to me by a Mexican graduate student at North Texas State College about ten years ago. He came from a small village near Patzcuaro in the state of Michoacán northwest of Mexico City. As a child he worked with his parents, brothers, and many other villagers in the potato fields near his home. A man came from Mexico City to organize these workers and make them rich. Everyone talked about it. He said many bad things about the priest, Father Bambalón. Father Bambalón was fat. This was so. Father Bambalón was lazy, very lazy. This was so, too. Father Bambalón was rich. The potato workers gave Father Bambalón much money. What did he do? Pray? Well, maybe.

The people began to wonder about Father Bambalón. They no longer laughed and joked when he came ambling by the potato fields on his big donkey. Some even looked darkly and muttered as he passed among them. It was whispered that Ruiz Alarcón, the man from the City, would soon drive Father Bambalón out of the church and dig up vast jars of pesetas that the Father had buried beneath the altar and return them to the people.

One hot steamy morning an inky black cloud gathered in the west just as Father Bambalón jogged up on his big donkey. The weather was bad. The work was hot. There was much anger. Suddenly a loud roar began close by. A large piece of cloud had fallen to the ground and was whirling toward the potato fields full of workers and Father Bambalón. A tornado. Work stopped. No one knew what to do. Some would run. Some would be on their knees.

Father Bambalón climbed down off his big donkey. "Peace, my children!" he cried. His voice was loud. Furious. "I will deal with this matter. I!" He drew out a long knife from a sack tied around the neck of his donkey. Then he turned upon the tornado and began moving toward it waving his knife. He was very angry. As Father Bambalón approached, the whirling cloud grew smaller and less black. It was not much wider than Father Bambalón himself. Then all of a sudden, with Father Bambalón slashing away at it, it disappeared. There was nothing left, just a thin white streak in the air where it had been.

Later it was learned that the cloud had struck the house of Antonio Moreles, where Ruiz Alarcón, the man from Mexico City, had lodging. Now Ruiz Alarcón lay bleeding in the plaza but not dead. Tourists took him to Mexico City, and he never returned. Once more the workers began to laugh with Father Bambalón, and the bad thoughts of communism departed from the potato fields.

Tornadoes will sometimes do things for no good reason at all except just to show off. One in central Kansas forty years ago managed to get the cast iron rim, or tire, of an old wagon

wheel around the trunk of a big cottonwood tree sixty feet tall
with a trunk a yard in diameter near the ground. Neither the
tree nor the wagon-wheel rim had been separated in the
process. My informant argued that the wind whipped the
branches of the tree together into a tall pole and dropped the
wagon-wheel tire over it the way you would put a ring on your
finger. This graphic evidence of skill could be seen in 1923 near
the town of Kimbrough. It may still be there.

Tornadoes, once they have settled down to business, don't
like to be crossed. J. Max Pullin of Rensselaer, Indiana, tells
the story of a Jim Bohanon, owner of a general merchandise
store at Dixon, Missouri. Bohanon was working near the front
of his store when a twisting wind hit near by. The suction broke
out the plate glass windows and was slurping merchandise out
of the store faster than Bohanon could ever hope to put it
back. He saw a bundle of brooms rushing by and reached out
to grab them. As he did so, a handsaw flew off the shelf and
sawed his thumb off. The moral to this story, according to Mr.
Pullin, is, "Don't argue with a tornado."

Some people, however, have not been warned of the tornado's stubbornness. Take, for instance, the Rogers family of
Stamford, Texas. In 1955 a tornado tore the roof off their house
and then stripped the wallpaper off the walls of a couple of
rooms. The Rogerses had the roof repaired and the two rooms
repapered in the same design as before. My informant didn't
know what this pattern was, but evidently it was something
tornadoes do not like. Next year another tornado—or probably
it was the same tornado paying a return visit—tore off the new
roof and new wallpaper in exactly the same way as the year
before. This same tornado also unroofed a gin and scattered a
lumber company that had had the nerve to rebuild after the
damage of the preceding year. But people are just as stubborn
as tornadoes. My informant tells me that the Rogerses and the
gin and the lumber company have again repaired and repapered. Their main difficulty now is to get tornado insurance.

Tornadoes in East Texas and Arkansas have turned cast iron washpots inside out. One in West Texas rolled up into a neat bale a three-strand barbed wire fence a mile long and left it at a rancher's front door. Another Oklahoma tornado neatly wrapped corrugated tin all the way around a small frame house under construction and then completed the job by dropping over the bare rafters a roof from a near-by house. The famous Waco tornado carefully remodeled a brick wall bordering the old I. and G. N. tracks between Fourth and Fifth Streets. Along a horizontal line four feet from the ground every sixth brick for an entire block had been removed and could nowhere be found in the debris.

This same Waco storm exploded one of the most widespread misconceptions about tornadoes. Many primitivists have credited the Indians with knowing where tornadoes would strike and choosing safe campsites. Waco as the home of the Huaco Indians had long prided itself on immunity from violent wind. It couldn't happen there—but of course it did. In defense of Indian wisdom it has to be admitted that Indians probably occupied only a small portion of what is now Cameron Park, and this particular area did not suffer from twisting winds. At Nacogdoches, however, a noted Indian settlement in East Texas, tornadoes have twice ripped almost directly over old camp grounds.

The photogenic Dallas tornado that appeared on TV earlier this spring was too busy with its public appearance to play many sly tricks. It did, however, lift an automobile over a two-story house and set it down again on the other side in perfect condition—tires, glass, and even radio. In this same neighborhood a house was completely blown away, all except a front room table on which a loose check made out to cash was found still lying undisturbed.

With all their accomplishments, there is one thing tornadoes have not been able to do: crash into polite literature. The only effort I know of (besides *The Wizard of Oz*) is the miserable

affair that collapsed the house of Usher. This wasn't much of
a feat. The place was already rotten and ready to fall. Any
minor wind would have done just as well, but of course Poe
had to have his pyrotechnics.

The tornado is probably a little too rough and wild for most
respectable writers. You would not expect to find it mentioned
in the pages of Shakespeare or Milton or Henry James or Marcel
Proust; but you may well wonder why our literary he-men like
Faulkner, Hemingway, and Steinbeck have avoided it—especially the first two, who hail from tornado country. Herman
Melville might have done another *Moby Dick* on tornadoes if
he had lived in the right place.

Naturally, however, the tornado is more at home in less
formidable literary circles. Mr. Boatright has pointed out to me
a doleful broadside in William A. Owens' *Texas Folk Songs*.
This ditty goes by the name of "The Sherman Cyclone" and
celebrates the terrible tornado of 1896. A typical stanza reads:

> We heard the crash of timbers,
> Of buildings tumbling down,
> Distressing screams of victims—
> Oh, what a dreadful sound.
> It would melt the hardest hearted
>   To hear them loudly cry,
> "Oh, God, have mercy on me,
> Is this my time to die?"

There may be in our vast tornado country many more such
picturesque local ballads. I should be glad to learn about
them.

The worst mistake tornadoes ever made was to venture into
New England. This they dared to do rather spectacularly in
1954, when a bodacious twister smashed Worcester and went
on eastward to knock at the very gates of Boston itself. Up
until that time tornadoes had been running wild all over the
rest of the United States, and people had been accepting them
—like measles. But not New Englanders. They immediately set

up a public howl and demanded that Congress *do something*. So now, through special appropriations to the U.S. Weather Bureau, the awful eye of science has been turned upon these murderous intruders. And justice is about to be done.

For the past year, three well-equipped teams of investigating scientists have been set up at Washington University in St. Louis, at Oklahoma A. & M. in Stillwater, and at Texas A. & M. at Bryan. These teams examine with microscopic detail the track of the twister, interview witnesses and victims, and study the spawning characteristics of the storm. An interesting sidelight of the Texas study is that Bryan and College Station, never before in the path of tornadic disturbances, have been hit three times since the investigating team set up headquarters there. The presumption of man has not gone unobserved.

The full results of the Weather Bureau's multiple investigation have not yet been announced. But the most significant work has been done with radar in spotting the development of tornadic storms. It is now possible for weather stations many miles away to locate a tornado the moment it forms and track it to its destination. Quite recently Professor H. L. Jones of Oklahoma A. & M. has devised and tested a method for spotting an incipient tornado thirty minutes before it pounces. He bases his method upon measurement of high-frequency electrical discharges from storm clouds in which tornadoes are about to form. A certain number of blips on the recording screen means that a tornado will be delivered from a thunderstorm in about half an hour. When perfected, this device should give everybody time to retreat to his storm cellar or "fraidy house," or at least to crawl under a bed.

Another interesting recent development has come about as the result of cloud-seeding and rain-making. Particles of silver iodide dropped or shot or wafted upward into a cloud apparently tend to de-energize it at somewhat lower levels. It cannot then build up the tremendous energies necessary for generating tornadoes. One pleasant but unsought result of the cloud-seeding program has been the virtual absence of both tornadoes and hail in the areas where clouds have been sown. The correlation is too strong not to be significant, but scientists still hesitate to make a definite pronouncement.

What it all adds up to is this. Man is on the way to controlling the weather, and before long tornadoes may become unknown except in isolated, sparsely inhabited areas. Every community will have its equipment—a cannon or possibly a guided missile—to deal with threatening storm clouds, and the tornado, we hope, will be shot dead before it is born. With the elimination of the scourge, a vast body of rude, uncollected stories will disappear from the memory of man. Let us rescue as much of this folk material as we can before it becomes engulfed by scientific progress.

The Prairie Dog

LANVIL GILBERT

WHEN the American white man came to the West, that direction toward which human progression tends to flow, a vocal and impudent little grazing animal was squatting and claiming grass rights over most of the area now known as the Great Plains. This animal, the prairie dog, existed in such great numbers, in such general distribution, that eventually he became as much a symbol of the American West as did the Indian or the buffalo or the patient cattle that lowed and grazed and carried life blindly up the trail to the slaughterhouses. His homeland stretched from the Rocky Mountains eastward to the western edge of the Mississippi Valley, and from Montana and South Dakota southward to Texas and northern Mexico. His protective instincts made him prefer treeless areas of short grass; through the humid prairies near the Mississippi Valley he was found less and less frequently, until between the 97th and 98th meridians he disappeared entirely.

In his western homeland—the only place in the world he has ever been found—the prairie dog was comfortable and prolific. His natural enemies could not seriously cut his numbers, so he was, until the white man came, well on his way toward demonstrating that animal life, if left to itself, will grow to the limits of its food supply. In Texas alone he occupied 90,000 square miles, roughly one-third of the area of the state. In 1905, federal observers found that one continuous prairie dog town stretched from San Angelo on the south to Clarendon

on the north, a distance of 250 miles. The width of the town
varied from 100 to 150 miles. A conservative estimate set the
population of this single colony at 400,000,000 prairie dogs.
It was estimated that a like number existed in the other favor-
able areas of the state, and thus Texas had a prairie dog population of at least 800,000,000.[1]

The abundance of the prairie dog was of great benefit to the
Indian. Because he lived in nature with a natural culture, the
Indian made whatever use he could of whatever was at hand,
and he found the prairie dog a pleasant supplement to his diet,
particularly in times of emergency when the buffalo was scarce.
The skins he used for making bags.

The Indians attributed great wisdom to the prairie dog,
apparently because its eminently sociable nature brought the
animals together in groups which resembled, as they stood
chattering on two legs, a council of government.[2]

Always interested in origins, the Indians had an explanation for the prairie dog's creation. It seems that long, long ago
a terrible famine gripped the forest. Both the Indians and the
animals of the forest were at the point of starvation. The Great
Spirit, wanting to help, announced that a great feast would be
held in the forest. Everyone was invited; everything was
invited. The Great Spirit prepared a huge animal and seasoned
it well. Then he hung it from an arrow which he had driven
through the logs of his lodge. When the guests arrived and
took their first bites, they began to cough; the seasoning was
bitter. Fearing they would offend the Great Spirit if they
excused themselves to go for water, they kept eating. They
were unable to suppress their coughing, however, and the
Great Spirit, almost deafened by the noise, interpreted the
coughing to be a lack of appreciation. In anger he turned the
guests into prairie dogs and cast them out of the forest into the
desert, saying that there they could cough without disturbing
anyone. He decreed that because they had been so rude there
would be no water where they lived. They left their beautiful

forest home and have never been permitted to return. And that is how the prairie dog came to be.[3]

The Indians also had a tale which explains why the prairie dog and the burrowing owl were frequently seen entering the same burrow. According to this Zuñi tale, it once rained so hard for so long that the grasslands were covered with water. Starvation faced the prairie dogs unless the rains were stopped, and they appealed to the burrowing owl for help. The owl located a tip-beetle, a creature with a highly offensive odor, and offered to feed him all of the beans he could eat. Then the owl instructed his wife to prepare huge quantities of an ill-smelling bean. After the tip-beetle had gorged himself on the beans, the owl had him exhale great quantities of air into a bag. When the owl released the fumes, the offensive odor drove away the clouds and the rain stopped. From that day on, says the tale, the burrowing owl has been the priest and friend of the prairie dog, bringing forth, hatching, and rearing its owl young in the holes of the prairie dog.[4]

A Southern Ute tale implies that the wisdom attributed to the prairie dog was not unlimited. In this tale the wildcat hoodwinks the prairie dogs into closing their eyes to play a game, and then kills several of them for its meal.[5]

The fertility which endeared the prairie dog to the Indian alienated him from the white man. Once the cattle industry had stabilized itself within fenced limits, the prairie dog became an expensive exasperation to the rancher. Since 256 prairie dogs in a year consumed grass sufficient to support one cow, the San Angelo-Clarendon colony alone destroyed annually enough grass to graze 1,562,500 head of cattle.[6] And because he ate not only surface grass but the roots as well, the prairie dog did permanent damage to the grasslands.

In the face of this serious economic threat it is something of a tribute to western man that he produced humor based upon the threat. In one tale an Englishman is said to have suggested that arsenical water be used to exterminate the prairie dog. The rancher informed the Englishman that prairie dogs do not drink water, which is true, but he added quite tallishly that they are instead so particular they take only milk—and then it must be fresh, direct from the cow. The Englishman then thought he understood why the white-faced Hereford showed so poorly as a dairy animal.

"You are hit by these clever thieves at both ends of the line; they rob you of both the raw material and the finished product," he said.[7]

Also told is the story of a rancher who worked for many years to pay out his small ranch. Then a prolonged drought was at the point of wiping him out, so he applied for a loan to carry him through. An appraiser came to the ranch and went over the land with the rancher.

"How many cattle do you have?" asked the appraiser.

"None," replied the rancher. "They have all died off during the dry years."

"Any water on the place?" asked the appraiser.

"No," said the rancher, "I have to haul it from seven miles away."

Just at that time a lone prairie dog came into view.

"Do you have many dogs?" asked the appraiser.

"No," said the rancher, "just that one. The lack of grass got the others."

Slowly the appraiser reined his team toward the prairie dog hole. He stepped to the ground and began slowly to roll the rancher's abstract of title into a tight cylinder. Then without saying a word he walked over to the burrow and began pushing the abstract far down into the hole.

"Hey, hold on there!" cried the rancher. "What are you doing? That thing cost me $45.00!"

"Yeah, I know," said the appraiser calmly, "but anything that can live on this section of land for three years without outside help ought to have full title to it."[8]

With perfect impartiality the prairie dog had an impact

upon the cowhand as well as upon his boss, the rancher. The cowhand was forced to alter his technique of riding because of the prairie dog holes. To prevent falling under a horse which had stepped into a hole, the cowboy laced his stirrups a couple of holes higher than was customary in non-dog country. This forced the legs into a jockey's position. Then when he pulled into a prairie dog town, the cowboy tightened up on his bridle reins, grasping them tightly far out on the neck of the horse. To insure against entanglement the reins were never tied together. When the horse hit a hole the short stirrups and tight reins "popped" the rider well clear of the falling horse, the tightened reins serving somewhat as a bowstring. In such a fall the cowboy suffered the occupational injury of "bunged-up shoulder" but rarely anything more serious; after three or four days of rest he would be back in the saddle.

An incidental result of this new riding technique was an upsurge in the number of mesquite casualties. Riders no longer had their legs free so that they could ward off limbs.

Soon the cowboy learned to let the horse have its head in dog country. The horse could sense the holes accurately unless they were "blind ones," holes long abandoned. An unruly horse was dangerous in the dog lands, so cowboys tried to pick a steady horse when working there.[9]

Because the prairie dog is not a dog but a rodent and a member of the squirrel family, the original and most common misconception about him is perpetuated every time the animal is mentioned. When Lewis and Clark discovered the animal for science on September 7, 1804,[10] while on their journey to the source of the Missouri River, they learned that the Indian name for him was "wishtonwish," the Indian approximation of the sound made by the animal.[11] The French, however, called the animal *petit chien,* or little dog. Lewis and Clark accepted the dog reference but added "prairie" to show where he was found.

Although the animal is said to produce edible meat similar

to that of the squirrel, the dog connotation has served effectively
to eliminate the prairie dog from the category of popular
human food.

From a remark which Zebulon Pike tried to imbue with
caution another misconception has flourished. After exploring
the Arkansas River early in the nineteenth century, Pike wrote
that he had seen a wishtonwish, a rattlesnake, a horned frog,
and a land tortoise all take refuge in the same hole; but he
added that he did not pretend to assert it was their common
place of abode.[12]

The idea grew. Father John Pierre de Smet (1801-73), a
Jesuit missionary to the Indians for forty years and a man of
unquestioned honor, reported that the prairie dogs admitted
to their dwellings the bird of Minerva, the striped squirrel,
and the rattlesnake.[13] This weird friendship between the prairie
dog, the rattlesnake, and the burrowing owl drew support too
from Benedict Henry Revoil, a French writer who reported seeing in 1865 over a thousand prairie dogs and a large number of
owls and rattlesnakes "sporting together with great agility."
When his book was translated in America, however, the editors
felt compelled to add a footnote to the observation: "If M.
Revoil saw this, well and good."[14]

Captain Randolph B. Marcy did not believe the prairie dog
and the rattlesnake to be friends, so while exploring the Red
River in 1856 he personally conducted experiments which
proved to his own satisfaction that the two were enemies. He
reported that in one case a rattler ate a full-grown prairie dog.[15]

The truth of the matter is now known: the prairie dog and
the rattlesnake are terribly frightened of one another. The
prairie dog fears for its own life, if it is a small dog, and if an
adult it fears for that of its young, considered a delicacy by
the rattlesnake. On the other hand, the rattlesnake will enter
the prairie dog hole for only two reasons: protection from
sudden danger, or a meal. The snake has come to know that if
he is observed entering a prairie dog burrow, the dog rallies

his neighbors quickly and they furiously set about to block up the entrance of the burrow, thus entombing and killing the rattlesnake. It is interesting to note that if a person throws a bit of dirt down a burrow which a rattler has just entered, the rattler will scurry to the surface in panic. But if the same trick is tried while he is in the hole of any burrowing animal other than the prairie dog, the snake will ignore the trick and will stay calmly underground.[16]

For those who want more evidence on the prairie dog–owl relationship, Lewis Wayne Walker, an ornithologist, can furnish it. In 1952 while observing bird life over a prairie dog town, Walker saw an eagle soar over. Several prairie dogs and an owl dashed for the nearest shelter and competed briefly for priority of entry. When the danger had passed all reappeared and went to their proper homes. Walker believes that an emergency situation produces an automatic truce.

While studying the nesting habits of the owl, Walker stumbled across an explanation of the rattlers that are reported to be heard in burrows. Walker dug over an underground owl nest and covered the nest with a sheet of glass. Then he set up a camera and recorded the hatching of the eggs. He found that baby owls, when disturbed, make a noise exactly like a snake's rattle. Walker believes that nature may have supplied this trick to frighten off intruders.[17]

Father de Smet innocently started another story. Noting that the prairie dog neglected to cut down certain plants, he concluded that he liked and preserved shade. It is now known that the prairie dog disliked and mistrusted shade because it harbored his natural enemies. Father de Smet did not realize that there are certain plants which the prairie dog considers disagreeably flavored, though he will eat even these when especially hungry.[18]

To counter the belief that the prairie dog digs his burrow to water, it need only be noted that the prairie dog is found in places where drillers have sought unsuccessfully for water at a depth of 1,000 feet.[19] To clinch the matter, the prairie dog in his native habitat simply does not drink water, having the ability to manufacture it in his stomach from the plants which he has eaten.[20]

Counterbalancing the popular misconceptions are certain truths about the prairie dog which are not generally known. Among the most interesting is the fact, discovered through laboratory observation, that the animal has almost no distance-sense. It is believed that through the process of reversed evolution he lost this faculty by long habitation on the plains. The process may again be reversed in the laboratory; several dogs of different ages acquired through practice a sense of distance perception.[21]

An even more curious oddity is that the prairie dog seems to have a magical immunity from injuries due to falls. Two owners of prairie dogs in captivity made independent observations of this fact. One owner noted that his pet dogs walked off tables, chairs, and window sills with almost equal absence of hesitation. This he attributed to their lack of depth perception, but he could not account for their failure to incur serious harm. On two separate occasions, five years apart, one dog fell twenty-two feet to a granite surface without apparent injury.[22] In comparison to the animal's height of slightly less than a foot, this is a tremendous drop. The immunity seems even more remarkable when it is noted that the animal has a solid and chunky body that would presumably fall hard, and it appears still more amazing when we note the improbability that such falls could occur in the animal's level homeland. And yet therein may lie the answer; perhaps the prairie dog *does* fall in a wild state. It may be that entering unfamiliar burrows of various and unknown depths during emergencies has taught the prairie dog the art of free-falling, so that he merely jumps and then relaxes himself into immunity.

Yet the immunity is not perfect. One owner reported that her pet, which habitually found pleasure in jumping down an elevator shaft, finally overreached himself and was killed in a fall.[23]

The prairie dog is a better engineer than he is generally thought to be. When the animal was numerous it was a common sight on the plains to see him repairing and reshaping with his jackhammer nose the mound around his burrow. But he is capable of underground engineering which permits him to remain high and dry in a hole that is filled flush with water. Besides his regular tunnels, he constructs additional lateral tunnels off the vertical main passageway. These laterals go upward to within six inches of the surface. As water begins to pour into the burrow, the dog scampers to the extreme end of his emergency tunnel. The water rushing into the burrow forces air up into the emergency space, forming air pockets which prevent the water from advancing further in the tunnel. In these air pockets the prairie dog waits out the flood.[24]

Not all prairie dogs thus supply themselves with air pockets, however—an indication that there may be mental differences in individual animals. Given enough time and water, a man can usually drown one out. The sly coyote has been observed digging irrigation ditches in V shapes toward a prairie dog's hole so that the next rain will bring out a meal.[25]

In his "wild" state the prairie dog is not very wild. He is an anomalous mixture of curiosity and caution. His curiosity compels him to admit foreign life to within a few feet of the burrow, but once a certain line of danger is reached he barks a warning to his neighbors and takes to his burrow. Although man usually hears him sound a high, short bark—hence the French name *petit chien,* or little dog—the prairie dog has a repertoire of ten different vocalizations: tooth chatterings, snarls, screams, chuckles, churrs, and several variant barks. Each vocalization has a special significance.[26]

In holes reaching a depth of from eight to fifteen feet, and having a horizontal length of from six to fourteen feet, the prairie dog lives out his strictly diurnal life. He emerges early in the morning and late in the afternoon for food and to repair his burrow. Midafternoon he spends in sleeping and caring for the young, which come once or twice a year in litters of three or four. At birth a dog weighs only half an ounce, but it grows rapidly and weighs about two pounds at nine months. When fully grown it usually does not exceed three pounds in weight, and average 10½ inches in height.

In captivity the prairie dog makes a good pet. He learns to come when called and to bark for attention. And although he seems perfectly content to be a pet, there is something about captivity which drives him to drink; he will accept water,[27] milk, and watermelon.[28]

When returned from captivity to his natural habitat, he immediately resumes normal wild operations with instincts that have been made no less sharp by domestication.[29] This wonderful adaptability is manifested in other ways. Once in Roger Mills County, Oklahoma, encroaching civilization forced a colony to move to a shinnery (oak scrub) savannah. Traditionally the dogs like neither very tall plants nor very sandy soil, but here they cut and pruned five or six acres of shinnery oak and sand sagebrush as high as they could reach.[30]

Another evidence of adaptability would seem to be the differences in hibernation habits of the animals at various locations. The Texas dog does not hibernate at all, though he is less active in winter than in summer. He does not store food but acquires a roll of fatty flesh which makes up any dietary deficiency which the winter imposes. In the extreme northern section of dogland, in the mountains, hibernation is necessary.[31]

But there is a limit to adaptability. The prairie dog could not cope with the poison which man found it necessary to administer in the interest of grass conservation. Thus the prairie dog, a native curiosity of the West about whom people long will continue to tell tales and misconceive notions, became, by mere loss of his tremendous numbers, a greater curiosity of the West.

1. C. Hart Merriam, "The Prairie Dog of the Great Plains," *Yearbook of the United States Department of Agriculture, 1901* (Washington, 1902), p. 258.

2. Reuben Gold Thwaites, ed., *Early Western Travels 1748-1846* (Cleveland, 1904), XXVII, 263.

3. "Miles-Square Housing Development," *American Cattle Producer,* March, 1947, p. 10.

4. Frank Hamilton Cushing, collector, *Zuñi Folk Tales* (New York, 1931), p. 269.

5. Robert H. Lowie, "Shoshonean Tales," *Journal of American Folklore,* January, 1924, p. 37.

6. Merriam, *op. cit.,* p. 258.

7. Horace Trout, "War Against the Prairie Dog," *Farm and Ranch,* March 8, 1919, p. 81.

8. John M. Hendrix, "Boils, Prairie Dogs, and Mesquites," *Cattleman,* July, 1947, p. 24.

9. *Ibid.*

10. *History of the Expedition of Captains Lewis and Clark, 1804-5-6* (Chicago, 1903), I, 73.

11. Walter Gore Marshall, *Through America* (London, 1882), p. 125.

12. Martin F. Schmitt, "Prairie Dogs," *Cattleman,* July, 1944, p. 18.

13. Thwaites, *op. cit.,* p. 263.

14. Benedict Henry Revoil, *Fishing and Shooting in the Rivers, Prairies, and Backwoods of North America* (London, 1865), p. 105.

15. Schmitt, *op. cit.,* p. 18.

16. Gordon Rose, "Prairie Dog Town, Texas," *Texas Game & Fish,* July, 1956, p. 23.

17. *Time,* February 25, 1952, p. 77.

18. Schmitt, *op. cit.,* p. 18.

19. Merriam, *op. cit.,* p. 259.

20. *Ibid.*

21. Burt G. Wilder, "On the Lack of the Distance-Sense in the Prairie Dog," *Science,* July 4, 1890, p. 108.

22. *Ibid.*

23. Marjorie Shanafelt, "Exit Friday," *Nature Magazine,* October, 1933, p. 184.

24. Horace Loftin, "Engineering by Instinct," *Science News Letter,* December 1, 1956, p. 352.

25. Bill Billingsley, "The Disappearing Dog of West Texas," *Texas Parade,* June, 1953.

26. Maurice Burton, "Studying Prairie Dogs," *Illustrated London News,* September 17, 1955, p. 490.

27. "A Pet for Plutocrats Only," *Literary Digest,* October 3, 1925, p. 55.

28. *Ibid.*, p. 58.
29. *Ibid.*
30. Ben Osborn, "Prairie Dog in Shinnery Savannah," *Ecology,* January, 1942, p. 110.
31. Rose, *op. cit.*, p. 22.

Almanac Lore

EVERETT A. GILLIS

ONE OF the least-explored sources of American folklore is the old-fashioned almanac, once as familiar to the American household as the daily paper or the annual seed catalogue. From the very earliest American printing until well into the twentieth century the common almanac was an immensely popular form of publication, and in its heyday performed an incalculable cultural service to generations of American citizens. In Colonial America, says one historian,

this humble vehicle of general knowledge was an honored guest at every fireside; the chimney corner was its throne, and its well-thumbed leaves gave evidence of the estimation in which it was held. Interleaved, it became a register of domestic occurrences and neighborhood happenings. Its predictions and weather wisdom were reverenced next to the sacred writings, and quite often it was the only literature to be found in many homes where its annual visits were anxiously awaited.

Throughout nineteenth-century America almost every interest and profession had its own almanac, including such titles as *American Almanac for Use of Farmers and Planters; Town and Country Almanac; American Anti-Slavery Almanac; Farmers and Mechanics Almanac; Christian Almanac; Phrenological and Physiological Almanac; Lady's Annual Register; State Almanac and Handbook of Statistics*. As the last of these indicates, it is in the nineteenth century also that one of the most familiar types of almanac, the statistical compendium, had its rise. Flourishing, too, during the century were the patent medicine

81

almanacs. *Haynes' Medical Almanac*, the *Vinegar Bitters Almanac*, and others advertising various cure-alls came regularly into thousands of American homes.

In many respects American almanacs represent an important primary source for folklore, for they preserve *in print* much contemporary lore that might otherwise have perished. Furthermore, they provide a means of pinpointing any given bit of folklore with reference to date and geographical location, and hence offer a valuable tool to the historian who is interested in tracing the development of folk belief. Moreover, the almanacs offer a rather wide variety of folk motifs: folk recipes and cures; proverbs—often couched in the local vernacular; lore on planting and harvesting by the moon and the signs of the zodiac; frontier folktale and humor; astrological prognostications. As one might suppose, not all almanacs are of equal importance as source material. One may read through a great many, as a matter of fact, before finding anything of value; but then he will occasionally hit a gold mine. The most rewarding are those slanted primarily toward rural consumption—since it is in rural areas chiefly that most of our traditional folk materials flourish.

Much of the primary work—that is, the actual collecting of the almanacs—has already been done for the folklorist. Although almost every large library has a supply of old almanacs in its archives, perhaps the chief repositories in the United States are the Library of Congress and the Archives of the American Antiquarian Society. In 1937, according to a brochure published by the Society, its holdings of almanacs and registers amounted to 20,000 items; and doubtless this number has been increased substantially in the two decades since. Numerous check lists of almanacs, particularly by states, also offer a further insight into almanac resources.

One of the areas in which the folklorist can profit by research in the almanacs is that of astrological lore. The widespread acceptance of popular astrology in the United States today is

due in part probably to its dissemination through many generations of almanacs. The earliest American almanacs imitated
English and Continental almanacs in carrying in their pages
astrological prophecies of various sorts. "The astrologer," says
Samuel Briggs in his *Origin and Development of the Almanack,*

ruled "destiny's dark counsel," and royalty itself often trembled before
impending misfortunes in the conjunction of the planets: pestilence in
eclipses, and death and ruin of kingdoms in the advent of a comet.
Astrologers, quick to take advantage of the popular superstition, began
to make political predictions; and prognostications were consequently
regarded as the most important part of an almanack.

Weather predictions, however, based on the aspects of the
planets, most interested American almanac-makers. A very
famous almanac of Colonial days, Nathaniel Ames's *Astronomi-
cal Diary,* which often reached a circulation of 60,000 copies,
may be cited as typical. Ames remarks in his 1727 issue:

As to what I have predicted of the weather, it is from the Motions &
Configurations of the heavenly Bodies, which belong to Astrology. Long
experience testifies that the Sun, Moon and Stars have their Influence
on our Atmosphere, for it hath been observed for Seventy Years past,
That the Quartile & Opposition of Saturn & Jupiter produce Wet Sea-
sons . . .

Here are some of Ames's predictions. For a date in February,
1737:

> Now Snow, or Rain, or Hail
> Or else the Planets fail.

For another, in February, 1744: "The *Planet Saturn* informs me
of Snow and Cold in the Winter Season; now for it, behold it
comes with a Witness." For a date in November, 1752, he com-
bines astrology with a bit of folk superstition regarding the
weather:

> The Stars and spluttering Lamp proclaim
> The near approach of snow and rain.

In its astrological predictions, *Leavett's Farmer's Almanack* followed the practice of placing at the head of each monthly calendar page a prediction for the entire month. Here is its prediction in the 1793 issue for the month of November:

November commences with two aspectal positions of the planets, Saturn and Jupiter, and Saturn and Mars, with the Moon in Capricorn, hence we may expect a cold, harsh storm; again, the 15th and 16th. Mercury falls low for the season, the 19th. The month goes out cold.

The most persistent phase of astrological lore in American almanacs is that associated with the pictorial representation of the zodiac in the front of most almanacs, namely, the Man of the Signs: a human figure surrounded by the zodiac signs, with lines drawn from various portions of his anatomy to the signs to indicate what area of the body each influences. It is in their wide acceptance of the lore of the signs that the folk have most fully adapted traditional astrology to their own uses. The signs are believed by many farmers to have a direct influence on common farm activities such as planting, harvesting, weaning, castrating, canning, and egg setting. In folk belief success in many of these activities depends upon the care with which the farmer consults the signs. Although the knowledge of the signs is a common folk possession in many rural areas, the almanac, as I have demonstrated in a recent article in *Western Folklore* ("Zodiac Lore," April, 1957), has played a vital role in its dissemination, since it not only holds the clue as to the particular date at which the moon will be in an appropriate sign, but quite often carries specific directions with regard to the activities to be consummated in each sign. This has been true from the beginning of almanac publication in America. For example, John Nathan Hutchin in his *Almanac for the Year of Christian Account 1753* hopes that "the Signs as they are placed will be sufficient to let the honest Country Man know the proper Season for gelding Cows, Castrating Sows, and breeding of Pigs; in the performance whereof I wish him good

Success." And here are typical examples from a contemporary almanac, the *Farmers and Planters Guide* for 1955: "All late beans such as Navy, Kidney, Pinto, plant in the sign of the twins in June"; "Flowers and Bulbs of all kinds are planted or transplanted in the sign of the flower girl"; "The best time to kill all kinds of weeds is to cut them when in bloom and in the sign of the heart"; "Colts, Calves, Pigs, Pups, and Cats are weaned best when the sign is in the thighs and the wind in the north." The reference to the part of the body influenced by the signs in the last two items, rather than to the sign itself, is a common folk practice, and frequently found in the almanacs also.

Another area of almanac lore is the traditional wisdom associated with the moon's supposed influence on the natural world. Both as a reminder of the dates of the moon's waxing and waning, and as a practical source book of current belief about the moon, the almanacs have done yeoman service to generations of American farmers. In this respect Robert B. Thomas' *Farmer's Almanack*, in the latter part of the eighteenth century, admonishes its readers to have an eye out to the moon.

April 13, 1795. A good time in the moon to sow hemp and flax, if your ground be not too wet.
January 5, 1795. Pork and beef killed for winter's use, to have it increase while cooking.
January 6, 1799. At this quarter of the moon cut firewood, to prevent its snapping.
August 19, 1800. *Mow bushes! mow bushes now!* if you have any faith in the influence of the moon on them.

The *Massachusetts Almanack* for 1795 urges its readers under January to "Cut timbers, if you wish it to last long, in the last quarter of the moon." *Bailey's Almanac* for 1821 reminds its readers: "It is said, when you want to gather fruit above the ground, the best time to plant and sow seeds and grain is when the Moon is ascending. But when you wish to gather it in the ground, the best time to plant and sow is when the moon is descending." An almanac called the *Weather Vane* in 1898 included the following little folk rhyme among its other samples of moon lore:

> When the moon is at its full
> Mushrooms you may freely pull;
> But when the moon is on the wane,
> Wait ere you think to pluck again.

Moon lore is not neglected in contemporary almanacs, to judge from the *Farmers and Planters Guide,* which informs its readers: "You will also find in this book the signs of the moon. The moon has a very important part especially in getting the ground ready for a bumper crop, in sowing seeds of all kinds, and all other work." And the editor then proceeds to give numerous examples of moon influence.

Historians of the frontier period of American history frequently cite the newspaper as a primary source of frontier humor. To newspapers may be added the early almanacs—sharers, as one might expect from their popular and familiar nature, in the production and dissemination of what Mody C. Boatright has called the folk laughter of the American frontier. Although the most famous of the almanacs dealing in homespun or extravagant humor were the Davy Crockett series of the 1830's, 1840's, and 1850's, other humorous almanacs also had wide circulation. The heyday of comic almanacs, according to Charles L. Nichols in "Notes on the Almanacs of Massachusetts," was the first half of the nineteenth century. Nichols reports that more than thirty varieties of comic almanacs were issued in Massachusetts alone during the period from 1830 to 1860. Some typical comic almanacs are *Broad Grins; or Fun for the New Year* (Boston, 1832); *Die Darkie's Comic All-my-nig* (Boston, 1846); *Elton's Ripsnorter Comic Almanac* (New York, 1850); *Food for Fun, or the Humorist's Almanack* (Boston, 1831); and *Sam Slick's Comic All-my-Nack* (New York, 1840). And one of special interest to Texans: the *Devil's Comical Old-*

manick (New York, 1837), the subtitle of which reads "With Comic Engravings of all the Principal Events of Texas (Millions for Texas! but not a Cent for Taxes!!)."

Although the stock in trade of most of the comic almanacs was current jokes of the Joe Miller variety, cartoons, humorous anecdotes, and brief dialect tales, many of them were simply burlesques of the serious almanacs: for example, Henry Wheeler Shaw's *Josh Billings' Farmer's Allminax*. Its chief humorous effect is obtained by misspellings. Representative of material in Shaw's series is his description of the Man of the Signs in his 1870 edition:

SIGHNS OV THE ZODIAK

The undersighned iz an Amerikan brave, in hiz grate tragick akt ov being attacked bi the twelve constellashuns.—*(May the best man win.)*

Following this is the conventional figure and a parody of the directions ordinarily given for its use:

KEY TEW THE ABUV PERFORMANCE

Tew kno exakly whare the sighn iz, multiply the day ov the month by the sighn, then find a dividend that will go into a divider four times without enny remains, subtrakt this from the sighn, add the fust quoshunt tew the last divider, then multiply the whole ov the man's boddy bi all the sighns, and the result will be jist what yu are looking after.

Occasionally burlesque elements are found in serious almanacs. The *Old Farmer's Almanack,* for instance, carried in its 1875 edition a take-off by Mark Twain on the advice to farmers traditionally carried in the pages of agricultural almanacs:

Turnips should never be pulled—it injures them. It is much better to send a boy up, and let him shake the tree.

Cows, in wet and slushy weather, should not be allowed to leave their rooms, otherwise a sudden attack of influenza may dry up their milk. Be careful, also, not to give them vinegar with their pickles. A simple diet of roast beef and potatoes, and rice pudding, is the proper thing to make cows thrive.

The pumpkin is the only esculent of the orange family that will thrive in the North, except the gourd, and one or two varieties of squash. But the custom of planting it in the front yard, with the shrubbery, is fast going out of vogue; for it is now generally conceded that the pumpkin, as a shade tree, is a failure.

An area of almanac lore especially fertile for folklorists is the category of folk wisdom, including superstitions, customs, proverbs, and weather sayings. The almanacs are rich in such folksay. A good example is weather wisdom; editors of almanacs frequently included current weather lore which readers had sent in or which they themselves had compiled from their own memories. I found the *Agricultural Almanac* of Lancaster, Pennsylvania, particularly bountiful in this respect. In a run of some thirty years, from 1870 to 1903, this almanac published fourteen items, ranging from brief notices about weather superstitions to complete articles treating the subject at length—typical titles being "Signs of Rain" (1870); "Weather Prognostics" (1877); "Weather Wisdom" (1883); "Weather Signs for Farmers" (1883); "Proverbs About Snow" (1888); "Signs of the Weather" (1900). In addition, this almanac carried inside its front cover a current selection from the *Centennial Almanac*—an astrological compilation of probable weather, and its effects on planting, harvesting, and other rural activities, for a hundred-year period.

Common superstitions frequently found their way into the almanacs and often elicited comment from editors, either by way of explanation or disparagement. The editor of the *Comic Almanac for the Year 1876,* for example, began an article entitled "Omens and Superstitions" with an *I-don't-believe-them—but* attitude, remarking: "I am not a bit superstitious, though I'll own I *had* rather see the new moon over my right shoulder." Then after citing a number of common superstitions—such as the danger of walking under a ladder, searching for lucky four-leaf clovers, avoiding spilling salt—he concludes: "I once shocked a good lady by laughing when her clock struck over one hundred times. [a sign of death]. 'You'll find it no laughing matter, and it may be in *your* family.' I was sobered at once; but no death followed this freak of the clock." The editor of the *Old Farmer's Almanack* for 1867 explains the reference to crowing hens in such sayings as "Whistling girls and crowing hens, often come to no good end" by pointing out that old hens past their productive age sometimes lay very small eggs no larger than pigeon eggs, containing no yolk, and often crow like a cock; and, he continues, "sometimes take on, in fact, the plumage of the cock, and practice his alluring fascinations." He had once read, he concludes his comments, of such a hen being buried alive in the public square of a European city after laying a small egg.

Though Ben Franklin was perhaps not the first to include proverbs in an almanac, he at least popularized the practice. In his *Autobiography* he explains how he came to incorporate wise sayings in his *Poor Richard's Almanac:*

Observing that it was generally read, scarce any neighborhood in the province being without it, I considered it as a proper vehicle for conveying instruction among the common people, who bought scarcely any other books; I therefore filled all the little spaces that occurred between the remarkable days in the calendar with proverbial sentences, chiefly such as inculcated industry and frugality, as the means of procuring wealth, and thereby securing virtue; it being more difficult for a man in want, to act honestly, as, to use here one of those proverbs, *it is hard for an empty sack to stand upright.*

Franklin's proverbs are interesting on several scores: they have both the salty smack of folk speech and the sly, gnomic qualities of folk wit. Moreover, although Franklin's proverbs are not original—being borrowed from compilations of famous proverbs —he so modified and rephrased them that they are essentially his own. Finally, through the popularity of his *Poor Richard's Almanac,* they re-entered the folk realm from whence they originally came, and became again part and parcel of the folk mind—to be handed down through oral transmission to succeeding generations like any other element of folklore. To see how well he succeeded in these respects we have only to compare Franklin's versions with the originals: for example, "A muffled cat was never good mouser" becomes in Franklin's styling "A cat in gloves catches no mice"; "Three may keep counsel if two be away" becomes "Three may keep a secret if two of them are dead"; and "Fresh fish and new-come guests smell by the time they are three days old" becomes "Fish and visitors stink in three days."

Research in old almanacs can be very profitable to the folklorist. If you happen to find a batch of old almanacs in your grandfather's attic, don't throw them away. These quaint, faded annuals are valuable source material to the folk historian patiently piecing together the basic pattern of American folk development.

The Mexican *Corrido:* Its Rise and Fall

AMÉRICO PAREDES

IT WAS the *corrido* of the Revolution that turned Mexican students to the collection and study of ballads. Except for brief mention in earlier works, Mexican interest in balladry began in the 1920's, toward the end of the Revolutionary period. Most significant works on the subject appeared during the 1930's, though collection of *romance* survivals in America had been done before 1910 by Aurelio Espinosa in New Mexico, by Vicuña Cifuentes in Chile, and by Menéndez Pidal in Spain.

The obvious *romance* ancestry of the *corrido* led students to overestimate the antiquity of the Mexican form, as well as its predominance as a uniform ballad type. At first an unbroken line was seen between the *romances* of epic themes and the heroic *corridos* of the Mexican Revolution.

The conquistadores had arrived in Mexico when the *romance* tradition was still strong in Spain, bringing the *romance corrido* with them, and thirty years after the conquest the Indians were composing *romance*-like ballads of their own. Two hundred years after the arrival of Hernán Cortez, in 1745, the colonization of Florida had been celebrated in *romances corridos,* evidence of the persistence of the *romance* tradition in New Spain. Then, with the war for independence, the *corrido* had emerged as a truly native form—speaking for the Mexican rural folk, singing of victories and defeats in the struggle against the Spanish Crown.

But the war with the United States produced a sudden

91

break. The attempts to oust Santa Anna after the American war, the War of Reform, and the French occupation produced no *corridos* which survived. The epic tradition ended, and the only *corridos* which people were singing in 1910 were broadsides about thieves and outlaws. With the Revolution the *corrido* again sprang into life and entered its second and its best epic period.

This theory about the antiquity of the Mexican *corrido* left some important questions unanswered, especially regarding the material collected in what had once been the frontier regions of New Spain: New Mexico, California, and the Lower Texas-Mexican Border—the old Spanish province of Nuevo Santander.

One question was the validity of the ballad hiatus supposed to have occurred after the war with the United States. Another was why the Lower Border *corrido* was in the ascendant during the period from 1850 to 1910 while in adjacent areas of Greater Mexico the *corrido* at this same time was supposed to have been at its lowest ebb. Still another question was why the *corrido* had not migrated into the frontier outposts in early colonial days, or why the *romance* tradition did not flower into the *corrido* in the provinces—in New Mexico especially, where the *romance* tradition flourished until very recent times.

Héctor Pérez Martínez explained the hiatus as the result of the shock of defeat and occupation during the American war, followed closely afterward by the French occupation—these events wiping away the memory of the heroic songs of the war for independence and stifling the ballad habit in the Mexican people.[1] Pérez Martínez' theory does not seem tenable if one considers that a folk may compose its best ballads in defeat. The Scots made ballads about the reverses they suffered at the hands of the English; on the Rio Grande Mexican folk groups made *corridos* about their conflict with the victors of the War of 1846. Mexican ballad students themselves believed that the Indians had begun to compose ballads thirty years after their conquest by the Spaniards.

Nor was there a satisfactory explanation for the relative recency of the *corrido* in the frontier balladries. In New Mexico the *corrido* never was an important native form, most of the better *corridos* collected in that area being Greater Mexican importations. The *décima* and the *verso* were the dominant forms, while the old Spanish *romances* were preserved. Some New Mexican scholars attempted to answer the question by overemphasizing New Mexico's cultural and physical isolation from Greater Mexico. When New Mexico was settled toward the end of the sixteenth century by Spaniards, the argument went, the *romance* and the *décima* had not given way to the Mexican *corrido*. After its settlement New Mexico remained isolated from the rest of New Spain, thus remaining "Spanish," as could be seen by the predominance of the *décima* and the *romance* in its balladry.

That New Mexican isolation from Mexico has been greatly exaggerated is recognized by Arthur L. Campa in his *Spanish Folk-Poetry in New Mexico*.[2] The emphasis on the "Spanish" character of New Mexico is relatively recent, obviously a reaction against Anglo-American prejudice toward the term "Mexican." Some other explanation was needed for the lack of a *corrido* tradition in New Mexico.

The biggest question, however, was posed by the Lower Texas-Mexican Border, where a local *corrido* tradition did develop. The *corrido* could be relatively recent in New Mexico because of earlier isolation from Mexico. One could suppose a *corrido* hiatus in Greater Mexico between 1848 and 1910. But the Lower Border *corrido*, flourishing during the supposed Greater Mexican hiatus, should have had an unbroken tradition stretching back to colonial times. The Rio Grande settlements were founded in 1749. If *corrido*-like *romances* were being composed and sung throughout New Spain in 1745, the *corrido* should have arrived on the Lower Rio Grande with the first settlers.

But such is not the case. As one works back along the

chronology of the Texas-Mexican *corrido*, one begins to lose
sight of it in the 1860's. It is not the individual *corrido* that is
lost when one goes back to the early 1850's, but the *corrido*
tradition itself. I have collected *corridos* along the Rio Grande
from men born in the 1860's and talked to other people of their
approximate age. Persons born in the 1860's and 1870's learned
their *corridos* when they appeared (when the informants were
children), or from older men of their own generation. They
learned no *corridos* from their fathers or their grandfathers.
Their answer to the question whether they learned *corridos*
from the preceding generations invariably has been, "People
sang *décimas* in those days."

In his monumental study on the music of the *corrido*, published in 1939, Vicente T. Mendoza, Mexico's foremost ballad
authority, was of the opinion that the *corrido* went back to the
earliest Spanish times.[3] Coming back to the *corrido* in 1954,
after a study of the *décima*, Professor Mendoza redefines his
position as to the *corrido's* age. The *corrido* as we know it, he
says, is a relatively modern form.[4] What students had identified
as *corridos* of the seventeenth, eighteenth, and early nineteenth
centuries were compositions in other forms. "The informative
press of the people . . . during the whole of the first part of the
last [nineteenth] century," Mendoza goes on to say, was the
décima.[5] He defines the effective life span of the Mexican
corrido as fifty years, from 1880 to 1930. The *corrido*, as an
independent form in Mexico, falls into three distinct stages:
a period of ascent from 1875 to 1910 (during which time the
ballad heroes are Robin Hood-like outlaws in rebellion against
Porfirio Díaz); a culminating period from 1910 to 1930 (the
epic period of the Revolution); and a period of decadence from
1930 to the present.

Mendoza's revised views on the *corrido*, applied to the evidence collected by other ballad students, make possible a
clearer picture of the history not only of Greater Mexican balladry but of the related balladries of California, New Mexico,

and the Lower Rio Grande. The rise and fall of the *corrido* among the more important folk groups of Mexican culture can be traced with much more certainty, even though some questions still remain without an answer.

In its epic period in Spain the *romance* was sung to a sixteen-syllable line, all lines making the same assonance for long passages, in the manner of the epic poem. Later the line was broken into octosyllables, and still later into rhymed octosyllabic quatrains with a refrain taken from the dance lyric. The *romance* without refrain continued to be sung, especially in Andalusia, where it was called the *romance corrido*—that is, a *romance* sung straight through, rapidly and simply. It was in its refrainless form that the *romance* seems to have come to America in greatest numbers. Gradually *corrido* became a noun instead of an adjective and the Spanish American name for the *romance*. In Chile, for example, Vicuña Cifuentes published in 1912 Spanish broadside *romances* collected from oral tradition, which the Chilean people who sang them called *corridos*.[6]

In New Spain the *romance* appears to have arrived with the first Spaniards. It was carried up into New Mexico, and later to California and the Lower Rio Grande colony of Nuevo Santander. Those preserved the best were *romances* on universal or novelesque themes—about unfaithful wives, incestuous fathers, stupid shepherds, and fabulous lands. There is some evidence, however, that a few heroic *romances* were sung until recent times, perhaps until the rise of the true *corrido* among peoples of Mexican culture.

The *romances corridos* underwent more changes in New Spain than they appear to have suffered in Chile, if Vicuña Cifuentes' collection is a fair indication of the Chilean type. In form the *romance corrido* of New Spain became less like the Spanish *romance vulgar* and more like the modern *corrido*. The subjects were preserved, but names, language, and settings were Mexicanized. These changes probably took place early, as the language and the habits of New Spain changed in response to local conditions.

Thus it seems that the people of New Spain, the future Mexicans, very early created their *corrido* form. But they did not use it, as far as one can tell, in new ballads of their own for a long time to come. The picture of the conquistadores making *romances* about their conquests in between battles with the Aztecs must be radically modified. The men of Hernán Cortez must have sung the *romances* that were popular at the time. But it is doubtful that they composed any *romances* of their own or preferred the *romance* over other current forms. Early examples of Spanish verse written in Mexico are most often *quintillas, redondillas,* or *décimas.* Some broadside *romances* were written in Mexico City in imitation of the eighteenth-century Spanish broadside, the *romance vulgar.* But the popular colonial songs dealing with crimes and other sensational events were neither *romances* nor *corridos* but *coplas,* satirical stanzas in a form that commented on rather than told about events.

The Mexican folksong for a long time lacked a narrative turn of mind. The Mexican's tendency toward lyric sadness or biting satire has been explained as the result of social conditions.[7] It is true that except for isolated areas colonial Mexico was a land of extreme class differences. The corruption of colonial governments led to cynicism among all classes. Nor did the situation change much with independence, which brought its continual coups d'état and generals like Iturbide and Santa Anna, who switched sides and ideologies when it suited them. Even heroic events were treated in lyric *coplas* or satirical verse. Calleja, the grim royalist general who was heroically resisted in the siege of Cuautla, is remembered in *coplas* like the following:

Ya viene Calleja   Calleja is coming
con sus batallones,   With all his battalions,
agarrando viejas   Seizing old women
por los callejones.   He meets in the alleys.

These were the first native Mexican ballads, it would appear. Behind the satire there is interest in events which were of significance to the whole population.

But already by Calleja's time another form was achieving hegemony over Mexican balladry. On the eve of his execution in 1811, the patriot Hidalgo wrote two *décimas* on the wall of his cell with a piece of charcoal.[8] The *décima*, a stanza of ten octosyllables with a rhyme scheme which usually is *abbaaccddc* (*décima espinela*), is found as a dominant native folk form in Spanish America from New Mexico to Argentina, from the Pacific coast to the Antilles. It now seems evident that the *décima* also was the dominant ballad form in Greater Mexico and on the Lower Rio Grande before the *corrido* superseded it.

The custom of glossing Christmas carols (*villancicos*) existed in Spain before the sixteenth century. Often these glosses were in *quintillas*, five-line stanzas. The Huastecan *trovo* of the Mexican hot lands still uses the five-line stanza as a gloss.[9] Manuel and Dora Zárate are of the opinion that the *décima* was being used by the Spanish folk before it was introduced into court in the sixteenth century, or that it was sometimes found in the form of two fused *quintillas*.[10]

In any event, the *décima* was introduced into court in the sixteenth century by Vicente Espinel, principally as a gloss for *redondillas*. It gained wide acceptance among literary men both in Spain and in America. By 1553 the University of Mexico, the viceroys, and the Church were fostering the glossed *décima* among the cultured of New Spain by means of prizes and competitions. By 1583 religious verse in the *décima* was being directed by the missionaries at the Indians. By mid-eighteenth century the *décima* was in common use in Mexico City, especially for political satire. By the end of that century there were men known as *decimeros*, popular makers and singers of *décimas*. The War of Reform and the French invasion (1858-67) were celebrated by *decimeros*, the most widely known of whom was blind Pascual Mauleón, an Imperialist.[11]

Crimes and wonders formed a great part of the *décima's* subject matter. The *copla's* tendency toward satire and commentary was continued, fostered by the nature of the gloss itself, which is a commentary on the *redondilla*. There were brief flashes, however, in which the *decimeros* caught the heroic spirit that the *guitarreros* later would give to the *corrido*. These occasions took place not in connection with the petty squabbles between generals but during times of foreign invasion. The *décimas* about Jarauta, the fighting priest who was a guerrilla against Scott's forces and who was executed because he refused to recognize the Treaty of Guadalupe, are more purely narrative than most others of their time. Jarauta himself is cast in the pattern of the *corrido* hero. He reminds one of *corrido* heroes like the Greater Mexican Benjamín Argumedo and the Lower Border Gregorio Cortez.

The Mexican victory over the French at Puebla produced some *décimas* which among the chaff of commentary contain little hard grains of heroic narrative.

¡Adentro los escuadrones!	In with the squadrons!
¡Machetazos de a montones!	Pile on the machete strokes!
¡De frente, carabineros!	Forward, fusileers!
En seguida los lanceros ...	And let the lancers follow! ...
¡Fuego nutrido! y ¡En guardia!	Heavy firing and on guard!
Qué batalla tan preciosa ... [12]	Oh, what a beautiful battle ...

Professor Mendoza, whose *La décima en México* is a definitive work on the printed *décima,* tells us almost nothing about the purely oral form among people of Mexican culture. But the works in *décimas* of Luis Inclán, the *charro* novelist and poet of the 1860's, indicate that in rural areas of Greater Mexico rancheros were celebrating their horse races and their roundups in *décimas,* as were the country folk in New Mexico, on the Lower Rio Grande, in Cuba, in Panama, and in Argentina.[13] Thus, for a period covering at least a century, the *décima* was the dominant ballad form among widely separated folk groups of Spanish America. Then, during the latter half of the nineteenth century, the Mexican *corrido* usurps the hegemony of the *décima*.

Mendoza believes that in Greater Mexico the *corrido* begins as a definitely individual form during the 1880's.[14] But before 1880 there were some signs of its emergence. The *décimas* about Jarauta had the spirit of the *corrido*. The War of Reform (1858-60), with its basic issues of religion and social betterment, produced *corrido*-like songs. One, written from the point of view of the *cristeros* (soldiers of Christ), contains the following stanza:

Ese tuerto de Salcedo,	That Salcedo, the one-eyed,
con su infantería lucida,	With his brilliant infantry,
iba flanqueando la izquierda	Came flanking us on the left,
para quitarnos la vida.[15]	To kill us all.

The Liberal side produced a ballad that is almost a *corrido*. It comes from Durango, one of the northern states, and was published by Vázquez Santa Ana as "El Corrido Norteño" ("The Northern Corrido"), apparently Vázquez' own title.[16] The "Corrido Norteño" still uses the *redondilla* and is full of literary bric-a-brac. At times, however, it sounds like a true *corrido*. It even has the beginnings of the *corrido* formal opening:

Amigos, voy a contar	Friends, I am going to tell
una horrible desventura . . .	Of a horrible misfortune . . .

One of its interior stanzas could have served as *despedida* or formal close:

Adiós, chaparral florido	Farewell flowery chaparral
de la hacienda de Avilés!	Of the Avilés hacienda!
donde peleó Regalado	Where Regalado fought
con rifles de diez y seis.	With number-sixteen rifles.

The French occupation gave the Mexican people a number of popular heroes in the guerrilla leaders who fought the occupying forces. The end of the war found Mexico filled with independent-minded local chieftains, many of whom had descended into banditry. In their bandit-hunting expeditions, Porfirio Díaz' *rurales* committed outrages against the humble village folk. On the whole, the condition of the peon worsened under Díaz. It was the men who took to the hills to escape Díaz' repressive measures who furnished the first heroes for the Greater Mexican *corrido*.

Class distinctions, however, were extremely strong, and the Díaz economy drew class lines even sharper. Most of the "better" people wanted peace and order at any price, especially if someone else paid the price. So it was the rebellious peon, the transported Indian, and the city *lépero* who swelled the ranks of the outlaw bands, and the Mexican *corrido* began not with a heroic period but with a proletarian one. The first *corrido* heroes rob the rich to give to the poor, showing their class-conscious origins. In them, however, are the seeds of the Greater Mexican heroic period.

The *corrido* must have begun in the rural areas and then moved to the broadside printing shops. As far as one can tell, the best of the Greater Mexican *corridos* of the proletarian period come from the provinces and were collected from oral tradition. Such are "Lucas Gutiérrez" from Jalisco, "Demetrio Jaúregui" from the Bajío region of central Mexico, "Heraclio Bernal" from Durango, and "Rivera" from the Lower Border fringe area of southern Tamaulipas and Nuevo León.

The Mexican broadside press seems to have turned toward the *corrido* at the end of the century. At first *redondillas* were used to continue a ballad begun in *décimas*. Then the *corrido* form appeared, though even some of the early Revolutionary broadside ballads were in *décimas*. The influence of the *décima* remained in the broadside *corrido* as a tendency to comment on events rather than to tell about them. The broadside press concentrated on broadside themes, of course—wonders, sensational crimes, and the like. When it treated the bandit or the insurrectionist it indulged either in extreme sentimentality or in condemnation expressed in particularly pejorative terms:

Parra ha pasado a la historia,	Parra has passed into history;
su tragedia ha sido triste,	His tragedy has been sad;
la sociedad ha ganado	It is a gain to society
que ese vándalo no existe.[17]	That this vandal no longer exists.

After 1910 (particularly after 1913, when the assassination of Madero plunged the country into general civil war) the epic period of the Greater Mexican *corrido* began. The old system crumbled, and Mexicans were divided into partisan factions in which class distinctions did not count. They became for two decades what the medieval Castilians were for generations—a warring folk in whom loyalty was seen as loyalty to a personal leader and rank was something achieved by bravery rather than by influence or birth. Broadside balladeers in the cities and rural *guitarreros* became absorbed in the same themes; their productions became less distinguishable from each other. Some ballads appear to have had a *guitarrero* origin, while others apparently were broadsides first and then were transformed through oral transmission.

With the Revolutionary *corridos* the ballad tradition of Greater Mexico reaches its peak. In the best of them a comparison with the *romance* is justified in the compact drama of the narrative and in the epic tone. These "robust and sounding verses," as Pérez Martínez calls them,[18] contain the spirit of the Revolutionary wars in greater measure than do satirical war songs like "La Cucaracha" or sentimental lyrics like "La Adelita," both of which antedate the Revolution in any case. The figure of Pancho Villa weeping for his Adelita owes a great deal to literate sources. The Mexican folk have seen Villa, who is one of the principal figures of the Revolutionary *corrido*, in the way he is seen in "La Toma de Zacatecas." Here he resembles the epic hero who rides up and down before the drawn armies, challenging the enemy champions to single combat:

Gritaba Francisco Villa: Francisco Villa shouted,
—¿Dónde te hallas, Argumedo?   "Where are you found, Argumedo?
¿Por qué no sales al frente,   Why are you not in the van,
tú que nunca tienes miedo?   You who never are afraid?

The value of the *corrido* had scarcely been recognized when various forms of pseudo-*corridos* appeared. Poets wrote local-color pieces in the *corrido* style, and musicians used *corrido* melodies as themes for their compositions. Some, hoping to do for the *corrido* what the Golden Age poets had done for the *romance*, produced verses that imitated both and had the spirit of neither. Those closer to tradition actually wrote some *corridos eruditos* about events that had happened twenty-five, seventy-five, or a hundred years before.[19] The *corrido* also lent itself to political propaganda.

After 1930, when Mexico's Tin Pan Alley took over the *corrido*, its decay was inevitable. At first radio and the movies employed folk singers and composers, and Mexican popular music had a brief golden age. But soon the demand for more and more new songs wore the folk material thin. A type of song was developed that is to the true *corrido* what American hillbilly music is to the British folk ballad. Perhaps the ultimate was reached when Mexico's double-barreled answer to Gene Autry and Frank Sinatra, the late Pedro Infante, groaned a pseudo-*corrido* into a microphone while a bevy of Mexican bobby-soxers squealed in ecstasy.

But the folk *corrido* has not completely disappeared. Phonograph record companies, which recorded much traditional music in the past decades, have helped keep it alive. Columbia's Mexican catalogue for May, 1957, for example, has a large number of traditional *corridos* on its record lists, along with the currently popular pseudo-*corridos*.

So can one trace the rise and fall of the Mexican *corrido*, a form distinct from the *romance* or the *romance corrido*, though descended from them, a form peculiar to folk groups of Mexican culture. There are certain things that the history of the Greater Mexican *corrido* can tell us about the folk balladries of the Spanish-speaking groups in what is now southwestern United States. For one thing, it is evident that there has been a much closer cultural relationship between Greater Mexico and the Spanish-speaking Southwest than was thought by earlier ballad scholars. The presence of the *romance*, the *copla*, and the *décima* in New Mexico and California (and the absence of the *corrido*), instead of showing a particularly "Spanish" culture in those areas, and their complete isolation from Greater Mexico, indicates on the contrary that before the war between Mexico and the United States the frontier colonies formed part of a Spanish-speaking ballad tradition that not only embraced Greater Mexico but the rest of Spanish America as well. This was a folk tradition in which the *décima* and the *copla* were the dominant native forms and the *romance* was handed down from European tradition. Isolation does not occur until the Southwest becomes American territory. The *corrido* appears in Mexico after this time.

That brings us to the phenomenon of the *corrido* itself, its almost sudden appearance and its rise to hegemony over other ballad forms. It has been noted that the best *corridos* of the Greater Mexican proletarian period came from the provinces. It should also be noted that the Lower Rio Grande area (the region now half in Mexico and half in Texas that once was the Spanish province of Nuevo Santander) was producing *corridos* of its own at the very beginning of the Greater Mexican *corrido* period. Where did the *corrido* begin its ascent, then? In Michoacán, as Professor Mendoza suggested in *El romance español y el corrido mexicano?* In Durango, in Jalisco, or in Texas?

The oldest Texas-Mexican *corrido* preserved in a complete form is "El Corrido de Kiansis," about the early cattle drives from South Texas to Kansas. It dates from the late 1860's or early 1870's, a decade before the rise of the true *corrido* in Greater Mexico. As "El Corrido de los Quinientos Novillos" ("The Corrido of the Five Hundred Steers"), this Texas-

Mexican ballad has been collected by Mendoza not only in the northern Mexican state of Chihuahua, but as far south as the state of Hidalgo. "El Corrido de Kiansis" appears to be the oldest *corrido* published in Mendoza's *El corrido mexicano*.

It is the Revolution that impels the rise of the *corrido* in Greater Mexico. The first stirrings of revolt against Díaz in the 1880's bring about the first outlaw *corridos* of Greater Mexico, but it is not until 1910, with the outbreak of general revolt, that the epic period of Greater Mexican balladry begins.

Border conflict, a cultural clash between Mexican and American, gives rise to the Texas-Mexican *corrido*. The Lower Border produces its first *corrido* hero, Juan Nepomuceno Cortina, in the late 1850's. By 1901, ten years before the beginning of the epic period of Greater Mexican balladry, the heroic tradition is fully developed in the Rio Grande area in such ballads as "El Corrido de Gregorio Cortez."

Professor Mendoza has suggested that the *corrido* began in musical Michoacán and spread from central Mexico to other folk groups of Mexican origin, carried by the *michoacanos* themselves, who have traveled all over Mexico and into the United States as *braceros*. From the evidence at hand, however, it is more plausible to believe that the *michoacanos* got the *corrido* from somewhere else, though they have enriched the music of the *corrido* through their undeniable genius. The same thing has happened in the history of European balladry; a musical, dancing people takes a simple narrative-song tradition and transforms it, the result being a kind of ballad that may sometimes be danced, a ballad with a refrain. In this respect it is interesting that the *corrido* with refrain is almost unknown on the Rio Grande, while it is pretty common in central Mexico.

That the Mexican *corrido* went through its first stages on the Lower Rio Grande Border—under the impulse of border conflict—is a thesis that could never be definitely proved. But it is one that is worthy of consideration. It has been noted that the Mexican *corrido* is a form with individual characteristics.

Special conditions bring it forth out of a continent-wide tradition in which the *décima* and the *copla* were the dominant ballad forms. It would be little short of wonderful if the *corrido* had suddenly come into being at two different places and two different times. Either the Lower Border *corrido* owes its existence to the Greater Mexican form, or the Greater Mexican *corrido* is indebted to the more localized Texas-Mexican ballad. Until true *corridos* are collected in Greater Mexico that go back farther than Cortina's raid on Brownsville and the cattle drives to Kansas, the theory that the development of the Greater Mexican *corrido* has been influenced by Texas-Mexican balladry is a plausible one.

1. Héctor Pérez Martínez, *Trayectoria del corrido* (Mexico, 1925), p. 16.

2. Arthur L. Campa, *Spanish Folk-Poetry in New Mexico* (Albuquerque, 1946), pp. 12-16.

3. Vicente T. Mendoza, *El romance español y el corrido mexicano* (Mexico, 1939).

4. Vicente T. Mendoza, *El corrido mexicano* (Mexico, 1954), p. xiii.

5. *Ibid.*, p. xiv.

6. Julio Vicuña Cifuentes, *Romances populares y vulgares recogidos de la tradición oral chilena* (Santiago de Chile, 1912).

7. Higinio Vázquez Santa Ana, *Historia de la canción mexicana* (Mexico, 1931), III, 24, 91.

8. Vicente T. Mendoza, *La décima en México* (Buenos Aires, 1947), p. 228.

9. Váquez Santa Ana, *op. cit.*, p. 45.

10. Manuel F. and Dora Pérez de Zárate, *La décima y la copla en Panamá* (Panama, 1953), pp. 20-21.

11. Mendoza, *La décima, passim.*

12. *Ibid.*, p. 400.

13. See for example Inclán's *Recuerdos del Chamberín* and *El Capadero de la Hacienda de Ayala.*

14. Mendoza, *El corrido mexicano*, p. xxvii.

15. Higinio Vázquez Santa Ana, *Canciones, cantares y corridos mexicanos* (Mexico, 1925), p. 225.

16. Vázquez Santa Ana, *Historia de la canción*, p. 250.

17. Vázquez Santa Ana, *Canciones*, p. 210.

18. Pérez Martínez, *op. cit.*, p. 18.

19. Mendoza, *El corrido mexicano*, p. 34: "La Toma de Papantla."

Chisos Ghosts

ELTON MILES

STANDING INSIDE the V formed by the Big Bend of the Rio Grande in western Texas are the imposing mountains known as "Los Chisos." This name, brought northward into Texas by the advancing Spanish civilization in the seventeenth century, once belonged to a tribe of Apache Indians. Since then, the name's use and meaning have changed. With the old meaning lost, several folk etymologies have arisen to explain the new. Nowadays, *los Chisos* is said to mean "the ghosts."

For at least one hundred and sixty years the mountains have been called Los Chisos. In 1787 a veteran Spanish Indian fighter of the north Mexican frontier reported, "I have ... discovered that Zapato Tuerto [an Apache chief] was attacked in the Chisos and not in the Sierra del Carmen."[1] Officially Los Chisos were so named in 1852, because that is what they still were called by Mexicans living just south of them in Mexico. With a U.S. government surveying party, M. W. T. Chandler passed with his pack train to the south of the Big Bend canyons. From the Mexican side of the Rio Grande, he reported that "this cluster, rather than range of mountains ... is known as 'Los Chisos.' "[2] If either the old Spanish soldier or Chandler heard that *Chisos* was supposed to mean "ghosts," he did not mention it.

Forty-seven years later was reported what seems to be the earliest published association of *Chisos* with "ghosts," by a

106

second government surveyor, Robert T. Hill. In 1899 with a beaver trapper and a Mexican interpreter Hill floated and dragged his boats down the Rio Grande from Presidio, through all the Big Bend canyons, to Langtry. Of the imposing mountains which he admired from the river, he wrote:

> The crowning feature of this desert is the lofty and peculiar group of peaks known as Los Chisos ("ghosts"). These weird forms are appropriately named. . . . The vertical slopes of the peaks, rifted here and there by joints and seams, give to them the aspect of being clad in filmy drapery. Wherever one climbs out of the low stream groove, these peaks stare him in the face like a group of white-clad spirits rising from a base of misty gray vegetation.[8]

In this account, Dr. Hill was the first also to associate the name *Chisos,* thought to mean "ghosts," with the physical appearance of the mountains.

But he was not the last. Also—they say—on moonlight nights the white limestone peaks rub shoulders with their igneous companions, like mountainous spirits among the darker crags. (Geologists say there are no limestone mountains in the Chisos.) Or, Los Chisos are said to be so called because of the spooky effect of the moonlight on their gray vegetation. Another reason is that on nights after a rain, the mountains glow with phosphorescent light. Patches of light may be seen on a mountain slope, or sometimes an entire peak will glow as though illuminated from within. Bob Clanton of Alpine says that one night, while on a camping and hunting trip, he saw an entire valley light up. For an instant, as bright as day, every cactus and rock stood distinct. Naturally, this is one of his most vividly recollected experiences.

Another kind of light reported is one that moves across the highest peaks and ridges. A ghostly torch is carried by the spirit of an Indian warrior stationed in the Chisos to guide other spirits to the Happy Hunting Ground. John Devenport of Alpine has heard that this light actually is not an Indian spirit light at all, but a star, seen only in the Chisos, that moves not over the heavens but horizontally and counterclockwise. But in this analytical day and time the horizontal star is explained away. There are those who say there are so many stars rising in the clear Big Bend skies that the illusion of a horizontally moving star is created when a newly rising star displaces its neighbor which rose but a moment earlier.

A final "natural phenomenon" explanation of the "ghost" association with the name Los Chisos is that when the first Spanish explorers saw these mountains the peaks were shrouded in mist. Because the vaporous clouds seemed like ghosts, the Spaniards named the mountains "The Ghosts," that is, Los Chisos. Therefore, so they say, *Los Chisos* is a Spanish phrase meaning "the ghosts." It happens, however, that there is no such word in Spanish as *chiso*.

Many know this, and then proceed to explain that the place name *Los Chisos* is a corruption of the Spanish word *hechizo*, which means "bewitched" in the fearful sense and sometimes "charming" in the complimentary sense. It is the second, rarely used, sense that almost always is appealed to when it is explained that *Chisos* is a shortened form of *hechizos*, and that *Los Chisos* therefore should be translated as "The Charming Mountains" or "The Delightful Mountains."[4]

Another school of thought has it that *Chisos* is an Apache Indian word for "ghosts" and that the mountains were named by Apaches who made them a hiding place, as they did the Davis Mountains to the north. The late Walter Fulcher of Terlingua, one of the first seriously to investigate the word's meaning, wrote, "I have heard certain clicks, grunts, and sneezes said to be the Apache way of referring to a disembodied spirit. None of them sounded like *Chisos*."[5] Confirming Fulcher, Apache language expert Harry Hoijer writes from the University of California, "The word for ghost is *t'ʃindi;* the *t'ʃ* is glottalized; vowels as above. This word is very unlikely as the source of Chisos."[6]

To depart from the "ghost" association, it is reported also

by Fulcher that *Chisos* was said by an old Mexican called El
Santo to be the Spanish plural form of an Apache word, *chis,*
meaning "clash of arms in battle." According to El Santo, at
night in the mountains "the clash of steel on steel" can be
heard "as the ghosts of Spanish warriors, killed in battles with
the Indians, come out to fight their battles all over again."[7]
But, writes Hoijer, "I know of no Apache word like *chis,* nor
any that has the meaning of 'clash of arms in battle.' "

Approaching nearer to what seems the truth about the name
of these mountains, an old-time freight wagoner named Tom
Burnham, who came to the Big Bend in the 1870's, told Walter
Fulcher that Los Chisos were named for a tribe of Indians.
Also, a Mexican regarded by Fulcher as quite intelligent and
observant "had heard that the mountains got their name from
a tribe of Indians, called in their own monosyllabic language,
Chis-sah."[8]

Further circumstantial evidence indicates that Tom Burnham and Fulcher's Mexican friend probably were right. It is a
fact that Los Chisos bear the name of a tribe of Indians, namely,
the Chisos, spelled also "Chizos." Some ethnological maps
place the aboriginal home of the Chisos Indians squarely in
the Chisos Mountains and the surrounding Terlingua desert
area.[9]

In addition, there is plentiful evidence to suggest that *Los
Chisos* is the Spanish plural form of a widespread Athapascan
(Apachean) language-family word which refers to the Apache
Indian and means "people of the forest." No dialect of Apache
has a plural form for the noun. From Chihuahua, historian José
Carlos Chávez, of the Chihuahua Society of Historic Studies,
writes:

We do not know the meaning of the word (Chisos), which shows at
once its native origin, and the whites must have called them [the Chisos
Indians] that because of some characteristic expression, which, although
not understood, fixed a term which in the future would be of use to them
in referring to the said tribe.[10]

This term Los Chisos, in reference to the Indians for whom the mountains are named, seems first to appear in writing about 1685 in a report of Lope de Sierra Osoria, governor of Chihuahua. In this report the governor for his own purpose classed the Chisos geographically with the Concho Indian,[11] and ethnologists have taken his word for it throughout the remaining two hundred and seventy-odd years. Thus the Chisos has been placed in the Utaztecan language-family rather than with the Apache in the Athapascan language-family.[12] In 1693 the report of a Spanish army officer, Joseph Francisco Marín, to the viceroy in Mexico City implied that the Chisos lived not only in north-central Mexico but also on the north bank of the Rio Grande in the Big Bend region.[13] J. Alden Mason—current authority for placing the Chisos as Utaztecan—writes, "It is probable that they were Apachean (Athapascan) in language," and states that he regards the Chisos as "closely related to, or a division of, the Toboso."[14]

The Chisos Indians were neighbors of the Tobosos and the Laguneros—both Athapascan—who lived in the Bolsón de Mapimi, that unbelievably cruel desert in Mexico just south of the Big Bend and extending in part north of it. Like the Tobosos, the Chisos lived on berries, roots, cactus, and reptiles, ate carrion (even bodies of dead people), survived almost without water, and worshiped nothing. Then they acquired a taste for horse meat and mule meat, and by 1693 were engaged in a war with the Spaniards, who wished to exterminate them. The Chisos strongholds were in the mountains of Texas and Mexico in the Big Bend region.[15]

As time progressed, the Chisos Indians lost their identity. Many were killed; probably most were absorbed by other Apache bands and tribes. It may be that the Lipan is the Chiso —his tribal name is *chishi*. At any rate, in May, 1715, the Chisos still were feared by sedentary Indians living near what are now Ojinaga, Mexico, and Presidio, Texas. They were listed as "enemies of the nations" by Major Don Antonio Trasvina y

Retis, in his plan for a trip from Chihuahua to Ojinaga. Implying that many Chisos lived north of the Rio Grande in Texas, the major spoke of their "entrances and exits" lying along his route. In 1766 Nicolás de Lafora reported that about two hundred peaceful Chisos Indians were settled at the Mission of San Francisco, near old Fort San Francisco de Conchos. Indicating that "gentle" Chisos had been absorbed by Apaches, Lafora stated that the Apache nation at that time was the only one hostile to the province.[16] Not until 1902 does the name seem to appear again with reference to a group of Indians. Judge O. W. Williams, in describing events of 1882, writes of "Chisos Apaches" who lived not in the Chisos Mountains but near San Carlos, Mexico,[17] in the Bolsón de Mapimi, the aboriginal home of the Chisos.

These Indians were given the name *Chizos* by the Spaniards. It appears that *Chizos*—pronounced in the seventeenth century as "chee-sos" or "cheet-sos"—is a Spanish pluralization of a local Athapascan Indian name, perhaps the Chiso's own word for himself or the name for him used by his neighbor, the Lagunero. Two Lagunero names for the Apache are *chïshyë'* and *tshishé*.[18] In northern New Mexico, Keresan words for Mescalero Apache are *chï-shë'* and *tsí-sé*.[19] Early Navajo words for the Chiricahua Apache of southeastern Arizona were *chí-shi*[20] and *tshíshi dinné*.[21] The Apache's word for himself is *shis-inday*, meaning "forest dwellers," which they called themselves from their custom of making their winter camps in wooded, mountainous areas.[22] And Harry Hoijer says, "The Lipan word closest to *Chisos* is their tribal name, roughly *chishi* (the last vowel is long; ch and sh as in *English;* the vowels are as in *ship* and *beet,* respectively). This might be the source of *Chisos . . . . Chishi* is said to mean 'people of the forest.' "[23] The Lipan Apache's region was west of the Pecos River and north of the Rio Grande.

Whether or not *Chisos* is a Spanish pluralization of the Apache word for "forest dweller," tradition is strong. When any but the traditional meaning of *Chisos* is suggested, the

reply is likely to be, "Well, I always heard it means "ghost.'"
This new folk meaning seems based on a localized Spanish
usage in north-central Mexico, found particularly in the Ojinaga-
Presidio area. In this region today, Spanish *chisos* suggests a
concept which until now has been translated into English only
as "ghosts." No example of the singular form *chiso* has been
observed with this meaning.

Leonard Wiley of Presidio observes that from *el hechicero*
comes dialectical *el chicero,* also meaning "witch," and that
from these arise *el chiso,* meaning "evil spell" cast by a *chicero.*
El chiso is a local Spanish term not infrequently used by Mexicans in Presidio and Ojinaga. Though this form does not mean
any sort of "ghost," it may exchange semantic influence with
los Chisos, which appears always in the plural form with the
plural form of the article.

Today the word *chisos* is used locally in Spanish to designate
something like a "savage, Indian-like bogy-man or spook." *Los
Chisos* suggests an indescribable but horrifying supernatural
menace with predatory Apache traits. Apparently the word is
used in this way principally by Mexican children, for as a child
Miss Delfina Franco of Presidio used *los Chisos* in this way and
heard it so used by her playmates. While her mother, Mrs.
Lucy Franco, has always understood *los Chisos* to mean
"Indians," the daughter says, "*Chisos* means something like
'bogy-man.'"

The clearest example of the more recently developed meaning was observed in 1946 by Mrs. Hope Tarwater at the picturesque and haunted adobe ruin of Fort Leaton a few miles
down the Rio Grande from Presidio. Mexican workers hired
by her husband, Mack Tarwater, spoke of mysterious white
turkeys they saw flying over the fort at night. When they moved
their cots from the spacious porch into the field, they explained
that evil spirits at the old fort had been turning their beds
around.

One day Mrs. Tarwater was at Fort Leaton with two Mexican boys, fourteen-year-old Chapa Brito and his cousin. When she saw them walking toward town, she called in Spanish:

"Chapo, where are you going?"

Chapo said, "My cousin has to go to the dentist. I am afraid to stay here alone. I don't like the ugly noises." His phrase was *los ruidos feos*.

As there were chores to do, Mrs. Tarwater reasoned, "I have to stay here by myself, and I don't mind."

Chapo replied, "But you don't see the *Chisos!"—No ve los Chisos.*—And away he went with his cousin to the dentist in Presidio, confident that his *gringa* boss was immune to visitation by evil spirits that assail the Mexican's peace of mind. But to Chapo, *los Chisos* were something that he could see, though vaguely, and that he most certainly could hear.

It appears, then, that there are folk etymologies and a linguistically observable etymology of *los Chisos.* Two folk etymologies derive the term from either Spanish *hechicero,* meaning "witch," or *hechizo,* meaning "delightful, charming." Actually, it appears that the Athapascan singular and unpluralizable *chishi,* meaning "forest dweller" and referring to the Apache, was adopted and pluralized by seventeenth-century Spanish adventurers as *los Chisos.* With the absorption of the Chisos Indians into other Apache groups, *los Chisos* lost its usefulness except as a place name—the mountains known as Los Chisos in the Big Bend National Park, Chisos Spring east of these mountains, El Vado de los Chisos (Chisos Crossing on the Rio Grande, known in English as the Comanche Crossing), and at least two localities in Mexico south of Ojinaga known as Chisos. Tradition, however, communicated the concept of *Los Chisos* as sinister, menacing, human-like beings, whose exact appearance, though Apachean, is unknown. The American, therefore, has translated *Los Chisos* as "the ghosts," but when he asks the Mexican to describe these ghosts, the Mexican cannot do so. The American would be stumped in the same way if he tried to describe a "bugger."

To support tradition there are many stories of witchcraft and ghosts with their settings in the Chisos Mountains. The stories of witchcraft have to do entirely with the protection of buried treasure by evil spirits.

Perhaps the long-lost hordes of silver came from the Lost Chisos Mine, somewhere in these mountains. It is said to have been worked by prisoners brought from the Presidio de San Vicente, just south of the Chisos on the Mexican side of the Rio Grande. Blindfolded, the prisoners were marched across miles of hot, rough country to the mine, and never permitted to see where they were going. Though none of the prisoners ever returned from the mine, there seems to be no legend current that the mountains are haunted by ghosts of these men who died laboring inside the earth. At this point, however, arises the familiar tradition that if one stands at the entrance of the San Vicente Mission on Easter morning, the first rays of the sun will strike the Chisos Mountains at the very spot where the Lost Chisos Mine is located.

At the foot of the highest peak in the Chisos, Mount Emory, is a "lost treasure cave" whose treasure is said to be protected by evil spirits. A long time ago, Spaniards with twenty burroloads of silver were attacked by Indians while they were coming out of Mexico. The muleteers raced into the Chisos Mountains for cover, but found themselves in a box canyon. The only escape lay in abandoning the silver and scaling the cliffs. Hastily they hid the silver at the base of a waterfall and climbed to safety.

Their intention was to come back at a later time and recover their cache. But before the luckless Spaniards could return, a rockslide buried the silver. Just where this silver is located, nobody is quite sure. It may be on Lost Mine Peak or it may be at the foot of Mount Emory.

Witchcraft enters the lost treasure story at the Mount Emory setting. It is said that a Mexican and his wife, trudging a cross-country trail to Presidio, once discovered a rich cache of silver bars in a cave at the foot of the high peak. Each lifted up two bars of the treasure, and they continued their march homeward, intending to return for the rest. But to the wife's sorrow, her husband died on the trail, undoubtedly the victim of the evil spirit in charge of guarding this particular treasure. The woman, however, brought her two bars of silver on to Presidio unharmed by the demon, and there told her story.

As the woman would not go back to that tragic place, others went seeking the treasure. They found that before their arrival at the spot the evil spirit had let the roof of the cave fall, covering the treasure with tons of rock. Incidentally, there actually is such a cave with the roof fallen in at the base of Mount Emory in the Chisos Mountains. As for the woman's silver bars, some disbelievers say they must have been only lead bars that had been intended for making bullets.

Tales of witchcraft in the Chisos have been used to support the theory that the name is derived from *hechizo,* or "bewitched." In 1953 Walter Fulcher wrote down a tale which runs thus:

When the Big Bend country still belonged to Spain, a party of men were forced to leave the Chisos Mountains and abandon a large amount of gold. The details are not clear as to whether these men had stolen the gold and were in hiding or whether this is connected with the more famous story of the lost Chisos Mine. It seems more clear that they had to leave because of danger from the Indians.

At any rate they hid the money in a cave. Now one of these men was a *brujo* or *hechicero,* a man who could cast spells or charms, and before they left the cave he made his incantations and cast a spell that no one could break but him. Invoking the Powers of Darkness, he fixed it so that no one could take the gold away until he returned.

On the way out the party was almost entirely wiped out by Indians. The *hechicero,* whose charms didn't seem to work against Indian arrows, was among those killed.

The survivors told the story, and later some of them returned. Others also tried to carry the gold away but the magic of the dead wizard still held. Some managed to enter the cave, but none could pick up the gold. Thus the mountain came to be called Cerro del Hechizo, which in time was shortened to *Chizo* and later applied to the whole mountain range and called *Chisos.*[24]

The story persists to this day. One old Mexican told me, with a perfectly straight face, that once while hunting deer he found the cave with
stacks of gold bars. But when he stooped to pick one up he was almost
paralyzed and couldn't straighten up. In terror, he managed to creep out
of the cave and never went back. Another old Mexican, now so feeble he
can hardly walk, assures me that with a rosary and cross and certain
words of prayer that only he knows, he can overcome the Powers of
Darkness and carry away the treasure, bewitched or not.[25]

As for the ghosts that haunt the Chisos Mountains, one
finds, as might be expected, that the area is frequently visited
by La Llorona, perhaps the most universal of all Mexican
ghosts,[26] the "wailing woman" who, after drowning her babies
in the Rio Grande that she might live a wanton life, has been
condemned to roam up and down the river for all eternity,
weeping and seeking the unabsolved souls of her children. The
reason given for the absence of human habitation in the area
of San Vicente is, "Nobody will live there because of La
Llorona."

Perhaps the best known purely local ghost legend is that of
Alsate, the last of the Chisos Apaches. This tale was first published in Fort Stockton by Judge O. W. Williams in a privately
printed pamphlet.[27] The judge heard the story in 1902 from
Natividad Luján of San Carlos, Mexico. It seems that in 1882
the renegade Chisos Apache chief, Alsate, was betrayed in San
Carlos by Leonecio Castillo to Mexican officials, who marched
the chief and his tribesmen into slavery in southern Mexico.
In an interview, Alsate's grandson told Glenn Burgess of Alpine
that his bloodthirsty ancestor fell before a firing squad in San
Carlos. Be that as it may, the rumor whispered among Big Bend
sheepherders and vaqueros soon was that the ghost of Alsate
had returned to his old haunts. The ghost was seen wandering
in Los Chisos and also in the neighboring Del Carmen mountains. Most often it was seen standing on some rocky point,
looking down upon the rushing waters of the Rio Grande.

Investigating Mexican officials discovered moccasin tracks
that led nowhere. In a cave they found animal bones, fresh

ashes, and a grass bed, all of which suggested somebody's hiding out there—but these were not ghost signs. Nevertheless, natives frequently saw the ghost near this cave. As the phantom apparently was harmless, officials stopped their inquiries, but Castillo, the informer, left the country in terror.

No sooner had Castillo gone than the ghost ceased to appear. With the spirit at peace, Castillo returned, but his neighbors again reported sightings of the restless Alsate. This time Castillo disappeared, never to be caught sight of again.

As James Cooper of Alpine has heard it, Castillo himself had a harrowing visitation. One night, traveling through the Chisos, Castillo made his bed in a roomy cave. As he lay on the cold ground, watching the moonlit peaks, he thought of his betrayal of the marauding chief. He laughed to think of Alsate's oath of vengeance upon him. Alsate was dead!

Then Castillo rolled over to view the cold form of the mountain on the other side. There, carved in its ridge, were the exact, terrifying features of Alsate's face. Castillo turned again to face the rear of the cave, to rid his mind of the illusion. Now he heard the winds shrieking among the rocks with the voice of Alsate crying out for his soul.

Rushing from the cave in horror, the informer ran to his house in San Carlos. Even here he was not safe. Whenever he ventured from the village, Alsate's spirit appeared. Day by day, Castillo grew more fearful and at length disappeared for all time.

The spirit world keeps no secret about the mountainous form of Alsate's ghost. As Los Chisos are approached from the north, Alsate's profile can be clearly seen on the right of the square-topped peak called Casa Grande. The mountain is said to have taken the shape of Alsate's face after his death, so that he might fulfil his vow of revenge upon Leonecio Castillo.

Two lesser known ghost legends have to do with Indians and bandits in Los Chisos.

The Legend of Cold Water Cliff, as told by Isidoro Salgado

of Alpine, deals with an Indian woman of the Chisos Mountains, whose baby unfortunately was born at the foot of the
cliff when the moon was full. The other women reminded her:
everybody knew that a baby born under the ill omen of a full
moon was sure to turn into some kind of animal—perhaps a
coyote or a lizard.[28]

The mother, to save her baby an ill fate and herself the
shame, carried it up to the edge of Cold Water Cliff. In her
arms the infant moved against her body as she listened to the
water bubbling from the rocks below and as she noticed on the
cliff the familiar paintings of deer and horses in red and brown.
She held her squirming baby with two hands over the cliff,
shut her eyes, let go, and closed her ears.

In 1954 Salgado and his brother-in-law were working cattle
near Cold Water Cliff. Here, says Salgado, "At night the wind
seems to be mysterious, because the running water is like
singing, when an angel is going to heaven."

After supper one night as the boys slept on the ground, a
noise frightened the horses. Salgado's kinsman told him, "The
horses are scared of something, because all the time I have
been working here, the horses have acted like something was
running after them."

Then Salgado heard a cry in the darkness. It was the scream
of a baby, as though it were falling down the cliff to its death.
Salgado says he has heard this wailing at Cold Water Cliff again
and again. "His crying lasts for a few seconds," he says, "and
then it stops."

Concluding, Isidoro Salgado says, "I did not believe in
ghosts, but I was scared. Now that I have heard this cry, I am
convinced that these legends that have been told are true."

Another tale, dealing directly with the origin of the name
Los Chisos, was heard by Lawrence Hardin of Crane. A caravan
of Mexican traders with mules and two-wheeled carts camped
one night by a waterfall and pool at the base of the dark Chisos.
These traders passed up and down the Comanche Trail dealing

in goods and slaves with frontier Mexican villagers in San Vicente, San Carlos, Lajitas, and Terlingua. While camped, they heard the wind's moaning between the rocks about the waterfall and knew the sound to be the ghost-cry of a girl who had died a violent death in these mountains. Therefore they named the mountains "Los Chisos," meaning "The Ghosts."

The girl was the beautiful daughter of a wealthy Don who kept an extensive ranch in Mexico. One day bandits descended on the ranch headquarters, looted the house, killed the old man and the servants, and seized the girl. They sat her on a horse and galloped away with her to the Big Bend country. As they rode in hot clouds of dust across the rocky desert, they boasted of how they all would take their pleasure from her body. The girl rode in silence and in tears.

After splashing across the Rio Grande, they took her to a hideout by a pool of water in a lush ravine. At last the desperadoes dismounted in the grove of live oaks moving in the breeze. The grass, the flowers, and the shade along the water made a luxurious world, foreign to the hot, bright desert only a few yards away. From the mossy rocks fell a sparkling waterfall, surging the stream into white foam.

The sweat-dripping bandits, white dust caked on their eyelashes, restlessly approached the girl, who sat exhausted on her horse by the pool. As the horse drank long swallows of water, one of the bandits put out a hand to drag her from the saddle.

"I am tired," she said. "So warm, so dirty. I am your prisoner. Only let me bathe. Then do with me what you will."

The bandits shrugged, joked, and let the girl dismount and approach the pool. As they smoked and bantered about what they would do to their beautiful captive, they heard her wade into the water.

After a time that seemed overlong to their lust, they strode to the water's edge to demand that she come out. There floated the dead, drowned body of the beautiful girl they had brought so far.

As the bandits stood amazed, a low cry came from under the rocks around the pool. It rose to a blood-freezing scream that bored into their terrified ears.

In shriveled fright, the bandits scrambled to their horses and fled, leaving the beautiful dead girl to float above the bright sand and leaving the rocks to howl her vengeance at them.

So it is today, when the hot day winds and the cold night winds twist and cry among the mountain rocks. It is Los Chisos.

1. Captain Don Juan Bautista Elguézabel, report to Jacobo Ugarte, Presidio del Norte, April 21, 1787, translated by Al B. Nelson in "Campaigning in the Big Bend of the Rio Grande in 1787," *Southwestern Historical Quarterly*, XXXIX (January, 1936), 213. The Sierra del Carmen is the next range to the east of Los Chisos, extending well into Mexico.

2. Chandler's report in William H. Emory, *Report of the United States and Mexican Boundary Survey* (Washington, D.C., 1857), I, 83.

3. Robert T. Hill, "Running the Canyons of the Rio Grande," *Century*, LXI (January, 1901), 381.

4. Presidio High School's Spanish teacher, Miss Eva Nieto, has always heard that *los Chisos* comes from *hechizo*, "charming." A few years ago, a Mexican government official from Mexico City emphasized this etymology in a speech which he delivered at the Big Bend National Park.

5. Walter Fulcher, "The Way I Heard It," MS.

6. Professor Harry Hoijer, University of California, letter, November 1, 1956.

7. Fulcher, *op. cit.*

8. *Ibid.*

9. Vito Alvessio Robles, *Coahuila y Texas en la Época Colonial* (México, D.F., 1938), p. 39.

10. José Carlos Chávez, Chihuahua, letter, April 17, 1957, translated by M. P. Slover, Alpine.

11. "The other nations lately in rebellion . . . have different names such as Chisos [in the Spanish original, *chizos*], Julimes, and others which it is impossible to remember, included under the apellation of Conchos, which is the more general name."—Charles Wilson Hackett, *Historical Documents Relating to New Mexico, Nueva Vizcaya, and Approaches Thereto, to 1773* (Washington, D.C., 1926), II, 221.

12. E.g., John R. Swanton, *The Indian Tribes of North America*, *Bureau of American Ethnology Bulletin* 145 (1953), p. 619. Swanton's

classification is based on that of J. Alden Mason, "The Native Languages of Middle America" and Frederick Johnson, "The Linguistic Map of Mexico and Central America," in *The Maya and Their Neighbors* (New York, 1940), pp. 52-87, 88-114. Mason writes in a letter, March 22, 1957, that his study relies heavily on Carl Sauer, *The Distribution of Aboriginal Tribes and Languages in Northwestern Mexico* (Berkeley, California, 1934), p. 63, where Sauer says, "The slender evidence that we have is that they [the Chiso] were a part of the Concho." Sauer's evidence is contained in the so-called "Parral documents," which is Hackett's *Historical Documents,* and apparently in the quotation from that work in note 11 above. Before Sauer's study, says Mason, the region "immediately south of the Rio Grande" was "formerly ascribed to the Apache." ("The Native Languages of Middle America," in *The Maya and Their Neighbors,* p. 69.)

13. Hackett, *op. cit.,* II, 395.

14. J. Alden Mason, University Museum, University of Pennsylvania, letter, March 22, 1957.

15. Hackett, *op. cit.,* II, 211, 219, 221, 335, 397.

16. Chávez, letter of April 17, 1957, citing *Documentos para la Historia de México* (México, D.F., 1857), IV, 146, 147, 160, and Nicolás de Lafora, *Relación del viaje que hizo a los Presidios Internos situados en la frontera de la America septentrional perteneciente al Rey de España,* edited by P. Robredo (México, D.F., 1939).

17. O. W. Williams, *Alsate: The Last of the Chisos Apaches,* undated pamphlet published at Fort Stockton, Texas.

18. Frederick Webb Hodge (ed.), *Handbook of American Indians* (Washington, D.C.), I, 67.

19. *Ibid.,* I, 846.

20. Mrs. Andrée F. Sjoberg, ethnographer of Austin, Texas, writes on February 16, 1957 that "an old book entitled A *Vocabulary of the Navaho Language* (Franciscan Fathers) gives *chi'shi* as a Navaho word for the Chiricahua Apache."

21. Hodge, *op. cit.,* I, 285.

22. Swanton, *op. cit.,* p. 328. Swanton also lists the Laguna names for the Apache, *chishye* and *tshishe.*

23. Hoijer, letter of November 1, 1956.

24. Just south of the Chisos Mountains, in Mexico, stands El Cerro del Hechicero Quemado—the Hill of the Burned Witch.

25. Fulcher, *op. cit.*

26. See Soledad Pérez, "The Weeping Woman," in "Publications of the Texas Folklore Society," XXIV (1951), 73-76. La Llorona recently has developed the habit of conducting her terrifying search at the city dumps of West Texas towns.

27. Williams, *op. cit.* In this and in other pamphlets, Judge Williams

makes it clear that he was associated with Lujan on a surveying expedition in the Big Bend in 1902.

28. This tradition probably is more Spanish and Mexican than Apachean. "Spanish Gypsies are terrified by the moon. They believe that a baby born in the moonlight may turn into some sort of animal."—Walter F. Starkie, British Institute, Madrid, in conversation, April 12, 1957.

More Chisos Ghosts

RILEY AIKEN

WILLIAM WEBER, often accompanied by his sons Ferdinand and
Phillip, made many trips into the mountains of the Big Bend
in search of Spanish gold. Once I, a skeptic and *algo desconfiado*
in matters dealing with buried treasure, went along with the
party in search of $70,000,000. We did not find the money, but
I came out with three folktales, one *corrido,* one chupaderro
stone, a rusty part of an old stagecoach once owned by my
uncle Dave Aiken, and a lead on a story I had heard as a child
in 1904 on the Alamo de Cesaria Ranch and stage stand. This
story was grand. Ghosts were legion and the tragedy was
Wagnerian.

Some day I hope to go into the Chisos Mountains again and
you may bet your boots I won't be looking for Spanish gold.
Instead I shall have a weather ear out for further details of
this story. Until I find them I am thankful for such *gajitos* as
follow. These bits I shall give you in Ferdinand Weber's words,
as he told them to me in conversation on August 29, 1930, in
Marfa, Texas.

The Bofecillos range of mountains is about eight miles from
the Rio Grande in the southeast corner of Presidio County. It is
said that the name comes from the Spanish word *bofes,* which
means lungs. Some say they doubt this since the *c* in the word
would have been *s. Bofe* can also mean fool, and if the word

123

Bofecillos should be derived from *bofe* then the range must
have been named for the kind of Indians who made their
home there.

Tradition has it that many years ago a trail ran through
this range of mountains from Chihuahua and that sometime
after the independence of Mexico from Spain much treasure
was packed through here to be hoarded in San Antonio. One
pack train was ambushed, and the guards and *arieros* were
killed and buried with the treasure.

Some years later strange things began to happen in this
region. Ghosts were seen, bells were heard, and flames of fire,
usually after a heavy rain, would flare from the tops of the
mountains. On Good Friday, 1927, many reports of ghosts,
bell sounds, and flames came from the Bofecillos. I was in the
mountains at this time with a party of four. One afternoon I
heard the bells. I listened. The sound ceased. There was only
the wail of a lone coyote out among the sotols. At the time I
was leading the pack mule at the head of the line traveling an
old trail Indian-like. I was worried. I knew I had heard bells
but preferred to keep this fact to myself.

"Could it be," I thought, "could it be that a buckle has come
in contact with the skillet atop the pack?"

I stopped, dismounted, and checked the pack. My friends
were more quiet than usual. I picked up a small rock and tapped
the skillet. Without knowing what I was doing, I looked up into
the face of one of my buddies. His face was solemn, his eyes
were large, and he was pale.

"That ain't it," he said.

"Bells?" I asked.

He nodded and spat on the ground.

Then I began examining our surroundings. It was possible
that the sounds we heard were made by the wind. In front of
us and to the north was a large, open draw, covered with large
mesquite trees and wild grapevines. All was still. And then the
chiming began again, and continued for seven minutes.

The men in this party, besides myself, were R. L. Ramey, one by the name of Stevenson, Vivián Luján of Marfa, and a Mexican from San Antonio.

Later, the same day, sometime between dusk and dark as we walked along the edge of a bluff of overhanging rock near our camp, my companions stopped and began to show signs of excitement. Naturally, I asked what was wrong.

"Wrong?" one said. "Don't you see what we see? You are a Jonah. What's the idea of the poker face?"

"The word of four against one," I said. "You win. Now out with it. If you are seeing things I'm glad, but what are you seeing?"

"Don't you see the fires? Spirits of the Chisos! My mama didn't raise me to run around with ghosts," said he.

Finally, as the night drew on I too saw flames, at a point some three-fourths of a mile away. They were silver white, about one foot in width and three in height. They flared up twice and I saw them no more. However, to the south about two miles I saw two more flares. One was green and the other was red.

My companions came to camp about eleven o'clock and said the flames were still visible.

Before making this trip I had talked to Father Palomo. He said that in the early days the Jesuits were able to find treasures and it was their belief that this could be done best during Lent. At this time the spirits of the dead who had been buried with treasure begged for mercy and their petitions were expressed in mystery fires.

Many ghosts have been seen in the Bofecillos. Some years ago a man who said he was hunting horses saw from a distance what he took to be a man seated on a rock. The horse hunter decided to approach him and to ask if he had seen any horses —one small bay in particular. Upon coming near this man the cowhand's horse began to shy. Finally he got close enough to the supposed man to make out that he was not a man at all, but a spirit-like something that spoke and asked what a rider might be looking for in those parts. The rider said he was looking for a small bay horse which had been marked with the PT brand.

The spirit said: "Never mind the little bay. Come with me and I will show you something worth far more than a horse." The mount got plumb spooked and began pitching and running. But the ghost, in the meantime, had caught him by a stirrup. Although by now the horse was running at full speed, the ghost hung on. It was dragged through thorn brush and stones and at last, in disgust, turned loose with this expression: "Vete, pues, ingrato; yo trataba de ayudarte."

Again, at another time, a man and his family were traveling by wagon on a road by where the ghost, whose name was Manuel el Curito, had tried to catch the cowhand. The family camped at this place for the night. After dark they became aware of the fact that someone was tossing pebbles at them. This noise scared the man and his family. They climbed into the wagon and sat all night listening to the pebbles falling on the wagon cover. Next morning they left and made good speed until they were well out of the Bofecillos.

Still again, near here, a cowhand rode up to a mulberry bush and was eating mulberries when he heard a woman's voice calling to him. And upon looking toward an overhanging cliff he saw an angel who motioned for him to approach. He did otherwise, and went yon to far places in great haste and left heel dust and the angel behind him.

Some years ago three Mexicans came into Marfa from Mexico. They hired a guide to take them to the scene of the Chisos treasure. They were digging one day not far from the mulberry bush where the cowhand had seen the angel when something made them aware that someone was watching them. Upon looking down the slope they saw six Indians mounted on fat ponies—two paints, two sorrels, and two duns. These ponies were bridled only with *bozales*. The Mexicans pulled up and left for Marfa. They said it was useless to dig for treasure so long as the spirits stood guard.

If the reader has no belief in ghosts I suggest he buy, borrow, or steal a horse and ride into the Bofecillos, make a camp all by his lonesome, stake his mount, eat supper, and then listen to the weird mystery of Chisos voices in the canyons, and watch for ghost fires.

Two Oil Tales

JIM ROWDEN

IN TEXAS OIL TOWNS and oil camps I have often heard the two tales that are presented here. They were always told as being true, with plenty of details and proper names, though the names varied from teller to teller. In my versions the names are purposely altered, so that no real persons may be thought to be involved. Whether these tales have any foundation in fact, I do not know; having been told and retold many times, they have now become folktales.

Fishing Job

A successful drilling contractor in Houston by the name of Bill Dublin had a younger brother named Charley. Little brother Charley was constantly in trouble. Following his discharge from the Army at the close of World War II, Charley had entered A. & M. College, where he managed to stay put until his G.I. Bill had run out. After this economic setback, Charley dropped college like a pair of hot tongs and embarked on an international drunk. Finding enough odd jobs to keep him in booze and trouble, he worked his way up into Canada and then finally back down into Mexico.

Big brother Bill soon got tired of collect telegrams and phone calls at all and any hours of the day and night, requesting beer and bail money. Charley, he thought, wasn't shaping up to much, leading this kind of life, and, besides, it was damned expensive.

128

To get some returns on his investment and also to see if he couldn't make something out of his brother, Bill Dublin decided to put Charley to work for him.

From the day he first set foot on a rig floor, Charley proved to be a big headache. Undependable and often half tight, he became the bane of tool pusher Red Freeman's existence. Red, a conscientious man, was very fond of his employer, but it was almost all he could do to stomach his boss's brother.

Besides Charley, Red was having more than his share of troubles on this particular well, which was located a few miles south of Galveston. They were drilling the well for Subsurface Oil Company. The rig was under contract to drill to fifteen thousand feet. During this particular time they had reached a depth of twelve thousand and had been plagued with every type of trouble characteristic of deep wells in that area.

Having just pulled all of their pipe out of the hole to change bits, the roughnecks were all standing around on the floor smoking and taking a well-earned breather. Red was standing over near the brake talking to the driller while his unwilling protégé, Charley, was at the opposite end engaged in a hot argument with one of the hands. Freeman was pleased that they had made the trip and had gotten their pipe on the bank without any trouble. "In between blow-outs, lost circulation, and stuck pipe, the only thing we haven't been hit with on this hole is a fishing job," moaned Red. Charley Dublin didn't hear him but the devil must have, for what followed in the next five minutes was enough to make Red Freeman want to give up the oil patch forever.

Charley's argument was over a game of washers that had taken place the day before while the men had a little time off during the running of an electric log. The other party involved in the argument was accusing Charley of extraordinary good luck in winning some fifty-odd dollars off of him and some other roughnecks in this particular game. In bad temper and slightly inebriated as usual, Charley heatedly denied this. "Why,

I could do the same thing blindfolded," he declared. "Watch this," and with these words he picked up a thirty-six-inch wrench and without looking tossed it over his shoulder toward the open hole. The entire crew stared in stunned disbelief as the wrench sailed some thirty feet on into the hole as neatly as if it had been aimed-in by a Norden bombsight. Red Freeman was stunned, too. He couldn't speak for some twenty minutes.

They failed to drill out or drill around the wrench. Fishing tool experts were called in, and the long, tedious process of fishing began. This was during the Korean conflict and the oil industry, like others, was suffering from an acute labor shortage. Because of this and also because he was Bill Dublin's brother, Charley was kept on.

Four months and $250,000 lapsed, and at last on a bright Sunday morning the "fish" was caught and banked.

This was a red-letter day for Red, not so much because of the fish, but because he had finally gotten the go-ahead from Bill Dublin to fire Charley.

The crew was taking the usual rest period after a trip when Red walked up on the floor to break the news to Charley. Charley was standing in his usual spot having his usual argument when Red walked up to him. Without any preliminaries, the pusher said, "Okay, Charley, you can go to the house!"

Charley stared at him a minute and said, "You mean I'm fired? What for?"

"You know what for," Red said with a smile.

"You mean this!" said Charley, as he reached over and picked up a brand-new red "thirty-six," and again without looking, tossed it over his shoulder.

The only difference was that this time it hung just a second, balanced, on the edge of the rotary table before it fell into the hole.

Fishing operations began again the next day, needless to say without Charley, who had departed for Nuevo Laredo, on a momentous binge to celebrate his new self-induced freedom from manual labor. Red was also missing from the scene. A man fitting his description was seen trying to peddle a used Geiger counter in a bar in Durango, Colorado, some years later.

Cabrito

During the depression there lived in the sleepy little Mexican town of Laredo an oil scout named Ralph Riley. Ralph had just gotten a wire from one of his bosses in Houston that stated he was on his way to Laredo to pay Riley a visit for the purposes of going across into Mexico and also of checking on an oil deal that the Hill Oil Company was greatly interested in.

Ralph, while more fortunate than many people at that time in having a job, was like everyone else in that he had a heavy financial burden trying to raise a family during those hard times. There had been no raise for him in quite some time. The result of all this was that Ralph was more than eager to put on a good show for his boss, whose name was E. O. Jones.

E. O. arrived as scheduled. One of the first things he expressed a desire to do was to go across the river into Mexico and eat. Jones proved to be a congenial person but manifested great finickiness in connection with his eating habits. Everyone has to be careful, of course, of how and what he eats in Mexico, but E. O. carried it to extremes, refusing to indulge in anything but cabrito, tortillas, and beer. He constantly embarrassed everyone during his three-day visit with the Rileys. E. O. insisted on eating across in Mexico every evening. He constantly badgered the waiters and went back to investigate the kitchen in each restaurant which they visited.

Much to everyone's relief, on the fourth day E. O. decided to end his trip with a visit to the Hill Oil Company fields in that district. After this, he wanted to stop by the Gómez ranch and attempt to wind up a deal which his company had been negotiating on for some years. Elizaro Gómez was the sole owner of several thousand acres in an area which the Hill Oil Company was greatly interested in and wanted to lease.

Although poor in a monetary sense, Gómez had consistently demanded what was considered a very high price during those times for his acreage. Through the years, Riley had become well liked by Gómez and the deal at last looked as if it was about to shape up. The home office had decided that the finishing strokes might need a master's touch, however; hence E. O.'s visit.

After the field inspections Riley and Jones arrived at the Gómez ranch about noon. Elizaro himself greeted his good friend Señor Ralph and was very happy to meet his *patrón*, Señor Jones. Asking them into his extremely humble adobe house, Gómez invited them to sit down and partake of the midday meal, which the rest of the family was already heartily eating. E. O. immediately had misgivings, for the inside of the house was anything but clean, and the large pot over the open fire had an ungodly-looking mixture of something that smelled to high heaven.

Realizing, though, that this was neither the time nor the place to exhibit his hygienic doubts, E. O. smiled graciously and sat down. The concoction in the pot proved to be cabrito stew. Although highly odoriferous, it was delicious. Jones couldn't get enough; he ate four bowls full, praising every bite.

After this unusually good meal E. O. felt expansive and expressed a desire to see the place. As they stepped out the back door another odor similar to the one in the house greeted them. This one, however, was almost overpowering. The two men looked around them, and on every fence, bush, and corral rail there hung a Mexican goat hide drying in the sun. Ralph remarked to Elizaro that he had certainly slaughtered a lot of goats. "Me no kill no gots," said Gómez. "They get seek and die!"

Without any preliminaries E. O. threw up. Mixed in with his second-hand cabrito on the hot South Texas sand lay any chances the Hill Oil Company ever had of finding any oil in Señor Elizaro Gómez' domain.

The Adventures of Ad Lawrence

F. S. WADE

In many American families stories about pioneer ancestors have been handed down from generation to generation, thus extending the family memory sometimes as far back as the seventeenth century. This memory is selective and constructive. It never retains a coherent history of the family. It forgets the commonplace and remembers the unusual, whether of incident or character. It will develop various forms, and will transfer incidents freely from one family to another. A check of family tradition against documented fact (where that is possible) will usually reveal deviations which improve the tales as tales and identify them as folklore.

The stories about Ad Lawrence, written by F. S. Wade, were originally published serially in the Elgin, Texas, Courier. The present versions are from a typescript furnished by John Poindexter Landers of Temple, a great-great-grandson of Lawrence.

A Hunt

IN 1824 AND 25 I* was living on my headright league in what is now Washington County just east of where Chapel Hill is now located. Both years were almost without rain. The Colorado stood in holes often a mile apart; the Brazos was not shoe-mouth deep. Grass had all dried up and blown away and

---

*In this story and the next, Wade attempts to tell the story as Lawrence told it to him. Hence the pronoun refers to Lawrence.

about all the game had left the country. Our only food was wild meat and fish. Our horses had been nearly all stolen by the Kaurenkerways and what were left were mighty poor. We were trying to keep our few cattle alive by cutting cottonwood trees and pulling down moss; occasionally we could kill a deer or a mustang, but our principal dependence was fish. We had no salt, and no grease to cook the fish with. It was a tough diet.

I noticed that every day about three o'clock crows came to roost in the cedar brake and they kept coming until nine o'clock at night. I felt sure that they went to mast [acorns], and where there was mast there would be lots of fat game. One day I was sitting on a stump trying to figure out what was to be done to keep life going in the settlement, for it was nearly Christmas. A little girl came up to me and put her hands on my knees and said, "Mr. Lawrence, I'm hungry." Her words cut me like a knife, and I couldn't keep back the hot tears. I went to my cabin, got my rifle gun, and shot a big black crow. Such a "caw-caw-caw" you never heard. Sure enough the crow's craw was full of mast. I called the settlement together and told them there was plenty of fat game where that crow drew his rations, and I was going after it. "As many of you as want to go with me, meet me here in the morning with the best ponies you have left." Sure enough nearly the whole settlement was ready in the morning, but I said enough men must stay to keep the Kumanchus from burning us out and murdering our women and children. So half stayed as guards and the rest lit out northeast, the way the crows came and went. Just after we crossed the Navasot one of the men killed a fat buffalo cow, and what a feast we had. This was the first time some of us had enough to eat in four months. We sent the horses back with three loads of meat to the settlement. Then we pushed on northeast as the crows were guiding us, for three days, when we landed in a sure enough paradise. It was a flat post oak country near where the city of Crockett now is. The ground was covered with mast and the woods were full of all kinds of game—bear, buffalo, deer, elk in hundreds. Some of the bear was so fat that they shook when they walked, and some that, like us, had just got in were lean as a sausage.

It didn't take a vision like the one that came to Peter to tell us to arise, slay and eat. Now I will tell you how we saved the meat as we had no salt. We cut it in long strips and hung it on lariats [rawhide ropes] or poles to dry. As soon as we had enough dried we sewed up the bear hides and put about one hundred pounds of meat in a hide, tied two together and put them on a horse, sending ten horse-loads back to the settlement by four boys and one man. The rest of us kept killing and eating and preparing more meat. In about eight days both the parties who had gone to the settlement came back leading every horse that could travel. A few days afterward, the whole party started homeward, every horse loaded with all he could carry. We all reached the settlement safely. Such rejoicing you never heard, for everybody had enough fat bear meat. We had saved the brains of our game. These we used in dressing our bear and deer hides, so that we could make moccasins, caps, jackets, and britches for the men and boys, and petticoats for the women and girls.

What a happy Christmas we had. Before our meat was all gone a splendid rain fell, putting the river and creek bank full; grass was hand high in a couple of weeks, our horses and cattle got fat, and slathers of game came back. Starvation time was over.

The Mustang Hunt

In the year 1828 the Kaurenkerways had stolen about all our horses. People was coming to the settlements nearly every day from the States and all needed horses. So I organized a hunt consisting of eight men all splendidly mounted and my nigger Jim for cook. We had a pack mule to carry about forty lariats and hackamores [halters], some axes, etc. We got our grub every day with our guns. We was going to the Gabriel

country, now Williamson, Milam, and Burleson counties, this
being among the best mustang ranges in the province of Texas.
Just as we made our first camp I saw a man on a long-legged
mule following our trail. When he came up he asked which
of us was Mr. Adam Lawrence. "That's me, young man; git
down, young man," says I. He shook hands and said his name
was Jim Jones and that he had got to the settlement a few
hours after we left. Said he, "I told the folks there I was from
Gadson, Tennessee, and that I was as green as a gourd; they
told me about your hunt, and said that if you would let me
go with you I'd get the green rubbed off." He smiled a smile
that would turn vinegar into honey. I said, "Impossible, young
man. We are going to an Indian country where we may have
to run for our lives. If that happened the Indians would sure
catch you on that mule and scalp you." Said he, "Mr. Lawrence,
you don't know this mule like I do. When it gets scairt it can
run like chained lightning. Now if you will only let me go I
will be mighty useful about the camp." Some of the boys spoke
up and said, "Add, let him go," so I said, "All right, but at
your own risk." Well, Jim was as good as his word about camp,
and then he could sing all the coon songs ever heard of, and
beat a circuit rider preaching. Well, we finally struck camp
on a little clear-running creek where there were lots of tall
elms near the Gabriel. [Uncle Add showed me this camp,
which was on Mustang about two miles below the present city
of Taylor.] We begun our pen, which was made out of elm
poles built eight feet high, enclosing about half an acre, a
gap on one side with brush wings widening out from the gap.
There were several herds of mustangs on the prairie, one led
by a big sorrel flax-mane-and-tail stallion. When he ran it
looked like he was waving two white flags. It looked like there
was more than a hundred head of them. So I picked this herd
and took one man with me every day so as to find out their
range. When the pen was built or nearly done I started out
to pick out points for the men that were to walk down the

mustangs. Just after we started Jim overtook us on his mule and said, "Add, let me go along." I had seen no Indians' signs anywhere, so I said all right. We were riding near the Gabriel. No mortal ever saw a prettier country. It was in May and the grass was as green as a wheat field. The south wind made it wave like the sea. There were patches of buffalo clover that were as blue as the sky, then spots of red and white posies that filled the air with sweet smells. Herds of mustangs off to the east, buffalo, antelope, deer everywhere. Jim was singing to himself a coon song that went like this: "Bend low, sweet lam, bend low."

Then we jumped a surprise. As we got to the top of a little hill we discovered about forty Comanche Indians in war paint and feathers not more than six hundred yards coming a-meeting us. When they saw there wasn't but three of us, they raised a war whoop and charged. Now I wasn't skeered for myself, for I could outride any Indian that God ever let live, if he knows anything about them, which I misdoubt; but I was scared for Jim on that mule. We struck out for camp at full speed. For three or four miles Jim kept up all right; then his mule began to throw up his tail. I hollered to him to get off that mule and get up behind me. He said, "No, Add, your horse couldn't carry us both. I think when the Indians get a little closer this here mule will get new life; but here, Add, take my watch and send it to my mother. Tell her there was no one to blame but me." The Indians were getting mighty close, so I said, "Farewell, Jim!" Two or three minutes after I heard an awful screeching and yelling, and my heart came in my mouth, for I thought they was scalping Jim. But they weren't, for just then I heard a pat, pat right behind me and I whirled back with my rifle gun cocked, for I thought it was an Indian; but I saw it was Jim, and you ought to have seen that mule, as it passed by me almost like I was standing still. Its nose was sticking straight out and smoke was a comin' out of it like out of a kettle. Its ears was laid back on its neck like they was pinned back. Its tail was a-sticking out behind it, and it looked like it was jumping forty feet at a time. I noticed three arrows sticking up in that mule's rump. As Jim passed me he hollered back and said, "Farewell, Add!" What was them Indians yelling about? Why, they was watching that mule fly. They turned back north. When I got to camp the boys were behind trees with their guns ready, but I told them that them Indians wouldn't foller us in the timber for they knowed when we shot we got meat. Jim had his saddle off trying to pull the arrows out of his mule. I roped its fore feet and throwed it and cut them out. I was a little careless when I let it up, for it made a bulge and away it went, looking back to where it had been introduced to the Indians. We never saw hide or hair of it again.

We spied around a day or two till we was sure that the Indians was gone; then we made our drive. We walked down them mustangs in twenty-four hours, got them all in the pen; and they was sure a fine lot. We found ten head of broke horses and mules that had got away from settlements, and a big brown horse with a Spanish brand that I afterward heard got away from a Mexican general. If it had been a white man's horse I would have sent him word, but I never mentioned it to that Mexican general, though I knew him well. We roped out about sixty, turning the rest loose. It took about two or three days to gentle our stock; then we tailed them six in a string and returned to the settlement, Jim riding the general's horse. We had no trouble selling out at from $30 to $60 a head. One day a man offered me five twenty-dollar gold pieces for the big brown horse. I looked at Jim. His lips was a-fluttering, so I said, "That is all the horse is worth, but Jim here lost his mule in the hunt, and I have been thinking of giving it to him, and now I have made up my mind. Jim, here is your horse." He shook me by the hand, the tears came into his eyes, but he smiled that smile again and said, "Add, you are white all the way through."

Your Uncle Fuller

About six years ago I* taught school at Crossroads in Williamson County. The place is now known as Lawrence Chapel. I had about sixty pupils, many of them older than myself. One of them, Henry Biggs, lived near where Elgin is now located, several at Post Oak Island, some at Thrall, others miles south; or in other words, my school territory was half as large as Bastrop County.

The neighborhood was half Baptist and half Methodist and not very harmonious. At that time the Baptists were noted for being good judges of whiskey and the Methodists for being artistic cussers. I am glad to say that there is some reformation among the Baptist brethren since then. I am not so sure about the Methodists. Hoping to harmonize the two factions, some of us organized a Union Sunday School. For a while it seemed as if the olive branch was going to flourish, but how often the best laid plans of mice and men gang aglee. In one of our scripture lessons that passage occurred in which it said, referring to John the Baptist, that his meat was locust and wild honey. All knew what wild honey meant, for there was plenty of it in the woods; but the locust was the rock upon which our peace ship was wrecked. The Baptists affirmed that it meant grasshoppers, the Methodists that it was wild locust beans. The discussion grew heated. When the Methodist circuit rider came to fill his appointment, the problem was submitted to him. He stated that from his reading of the Hebrew scriptures he concluded "beans" was meant. When the Baptist preacher filled his appointment the issue was submitted to him, and he stated that the Greek testament indicated that grasshoppers was meant. Then the war was on.

I would like to say in parentheses, understand, that from the way these preachers murdered the English language in their pulpits, I then thought their knowledge of Hebrew and Greek was about equal to my acquaintance with Sanskrit.

*The narrator here is Wade; the event took place about 1870.

I was sleeping in the west room at Uncle Add's one night, when I was aroused by loud cursing and yelling at the front gate. He hurried in with a big buffalo gun in his hand and said, "Fell" — he always called me Fell — "have you got any powder?" Said I, "What's the matter?" "Why, the grasshoppers have swarmed and have been to Lexington, where they have got bad whiskey. Now they have come for a fight, and they're going to get it!" He emptied my little pistol flask of powder, put a patch over the muzzle of the big gun, then rammed down a slug as big as a pullet's egg, and slipped on a cap. As he started for the front gallery, one of the belligerents yelled out, "Is Edmund there?" This was Uncle Add's oldest son. "Naw, but your Uncle Fuller is." As he pulled the hammer of that big gun it clicked three times, and the sound could have been heard a hundred yards away. Away went the grasshoppers at full speed. The old man set his gun against the wall, and remarked, "They knew what was a-coming. I am proud that they didn't stay." At the end of the lane about one hundred yards south of the house a large post oak leaned over the road. We heard a fall as the flying besiegers reached it, and someone groaned. A day or two after we heard that a young man had been hauled to Lexington for medical treatment, having been thrown off his horse in a roundup. Uncle Add sent me over to tell his folks to bring that boy home where his mommy could nurse him; that he would not trouble them with his gun or with the law, and that he was done if they were. So ended the grasshopper versus the bean war.

The Quarrel

Adam Lawrence was one of Austin's first colonists. He located his headright league and labor of land near the Brazos River, part of it being beautiful, smooth prairie, the balance a cedar brake, with a beautiful spring creek running through the princely domain.

For many years he prospered greatly here, but after a while other settlers, seeing the desirability of the location, formed a thriving neighborhood. This did not suit Uncle Add; he said that people were getting too thick, so he traded this splendid estate with all its improvements for a horse to run mustangs with, and with two friends, Jim Jones to whom I introduced you to in the Mustang hunt, and another kindred spirit, they moved to Newyears Creek, where game was plentiful and grass good. Here they opened up little farms, and all went well for a year or two; but suddenly appalling disaster overtook them. One morning in corn plowing time they found that the Indians had stolen every horse they had the night before.

When they met to discuss plans for the recovery of their stock, Uncle Add said, "Boys, what shall we do?" His two friends proposed to go to the settlements twenty miles away for help and horses.

"No," said Uncle Add, "by the time we could accomplish that our horses would be so far away that we could never overtake them. My plan is for each of us to start at once on foot, taking some dried meat and a gourd of water."

To this plan his friends would not agree. The discussion became heated, and such words as "fool," "coward," and the like were freely used.

At last Uncle Add said, "As for me, I am going to strike the trail at once." So they parted in anger, two returning to the settlements for help, the other striking the trail. He said that for years he had lived on wild meat exclusively and that a man living on that kind of food was never sick, and that he could run all day. He was sure that he ran and walked sixty miles, though he got a late start, before night overtook him. He had passed their first camp and was sure there were but three of the thieves.

Before night of the next day he came in sight of the stolen herd, but had to keep out of sight until dark. At dark he saw the three Indians staking out the horses in a little prairie glade. After it was fully dark he stealthily crawled up to the horses, necked and tailed the whole bunch, and led them about three miles on the back trail as near as he could find it, though it was very dark. Then he stopped and sat down in the grass. The longer he sat the madder he got.

At last he looked to the priming of his flintlock gun, hitched the horses, and began a still hunt for his enemies. With the silence of the trained frontiersman, he searched one thicket after another until at last he was rewarded by seeing a dim light in a dense thicket. With infinite skill and patience he crawled close enough to see, by the dim light of the fire, two of his enemies lying on the ground asleep; the third was sitting humped up over half awake with his back to a tree. Slowly he approached, when suddenly the half-awake Indian sprang up. Whether he heard the stealthy approach of his enemy or smelled him will never be known, for an unerring rifle ball struck him between the eyes.

In an instant a second Indian was struck dead with the huge butcher knife; but the third one lunged in the bushes and made his escape. Uncle Add said, "That Indian was sure scairt." For three hundred yards he could hear him falling over logs, running against trees and brush.

After reloading his gun he scalped the two fallen foes, took such of their plunder as he could use, piled the balance on the fire, then returned to the horses.

The next evening he met his two neighbors and six other men, all well-mounted. Of course these people expressed their wonder and admiration for his bravery and skill, after he had shown his trophies and they had seen the recovered horses.

His two neighbors hung back in the rear. At last Uncle Add said, "Boys, you did what you thought was best." Then Jim Jones came up with a curious look on his face and his lips "sorter a-fluttering," and said, "Add Lawrence, don't you ever ask me again what to do in the time of trouble, but tell me what I must do and I will do it or die trying." His other neighbor said, "Them is my sentiments." So the three neighbors shook hands and were friends ever afterward.

The Old Spaniard

In 1833 Uncle Add Lawrence was living on a ranch west of the Brazos River engaged in stock raising and mustang hunting. One day an old Spaniard walked up to the cabin stating that he was sick, and asked that he might stay a few days to rest. Uncle Add said he was afraid of him the first time he saw him, but he never turned anyone away in distress.

In about a month the old Spaniard seemed fully recovered. One day he told Uncle Add that he was one of Lafitte's buccaneers; that he had helped scuttle many a ship and rob many a town on the Spanish Main, and that when Lafitte was captured on Galveston Island by U.S. Marines and all his ships burned, he and two companions were guarding the treasure some distance from the scene of the surrender. After the victorious fleet of U.S. ships sailed away with their prisoners, they placed the treasure in two small cannons, one filled with silver, the other with gold, buried them in the sand four feet deep, marking a hackberry tree and measuring the distance to the treasure, then solemnly swearing that neither would ever try to recover the treasure unless all three were together. They then made their escape, one going to Mexico, the others to New Orleans.

"Now," said the old Spaniard, "I have learned that my two companions are dead, so I am released from my oath and am on my way to recover the money. If you, señor, will go and help me you shall have one-half, and if you will give me a home as long as I live, you shall be my heir."

Preparations for the trip were made at once. When they were ready to start, Uncle Add furnished a horse for each of them, but the old man said, "No, señor, I never rode a horse and never will. You ride and I will walk." The second night's camp was on the prairie. A full moon was shining brightly. Uncle Add said he could not sleep. After a while he looked at the old Spaniard, who was sleeping on his back, his shirt open in front. He saw a great scar across the man's breast, and his face had many scars on it.

Suddenly he said it came to him that his companion was not a mortal but the devil, leading him to destruction. While looking in horror upon the scarred sleeper he heard an owl hoot in a near-by bottom; a timber wolf uttered a doleful howl, then the heavens seemed to be on fire and the stars fell in showers. [Children, ask your parents to tell you about the falling of the stars in the year 1833, November 3.]

He sprang on his horse and fled for home, reaching there the next day, so badly frightened that he could neither eat or sleep for a day or two.

About a month afterward he got a message from a man who lived on Simms Bayou, that the day after the falling of the stars an old sick Spaniard came to his cabin and died in a few days. Before the end the old man gave him a package to give to his heir, Señor Adam Lawrence.

The package, on being opened, contained some Spanish gold and a map of Galveston Island, a tree and 703 varas giving the direction. This he handed to his wife, Aunt Sallie, to put away carefully. Then he wrote to his brother-in-law, Lindsay P. Rucker, who was a surveyor and lived in what is now known as Burleson County to bring his surveyor's instruments and his son as soon as possible. On the arrival of the surveyor and the telling of the tale of treasure, preparations for the hunt were soon complete, but Aunt Sallie forgot where she put the map and a long hunt proved unsuccessful. All any of them could remember was that the tree was 703 varas, but what direction all had forgotten.

The party crossed the bay and found the hackberry tree. They then measured 703 varas, and commenced punching rods in the sand. This they kept up in a circle until their provisions gave out, finding nothing. Several other unavailing trips were made.

The old Spaniard evidently told the truth, for many years afterward a great storm on the island washed up an old cannon filled with silver. If the other filled with gold was ever found, I have never heard of it. Doubtless it lies buried where the buccaneers placed it.

Old Man Banxton

The man I am going to write about would be a unique character in these days, but his kind in the days before the War Between the States was very common. He was a little old man, stoop-shouldered, no education, but very honest and in this particular he measured every other's corn in his half bushel. He wronged no one, nor permitted anyone to wrong him and live. He was the grandfather of Mr. Jim Banxton who lives south of town.

Conditions in those days were very different from these times. Then I never heard of a mortgage, or of anyone paying interest on borrowed money, or taking a note. If a man tried to beat his honest debts, he was so completely ostracized that he had to move. People's wants were very few, and though the crops often failed, there was plenty of fat cattle on the prairie and always fat hogs in the woods in winter. Nearly all the wearing apparel was made at home, except for one pair of shoes for each member of the family once a year. The girls usually got one calico and one lawn dress a year.

When you took your sweetheart to a party or to church, her mother or father saddled her pony, and away you rode as happy as the day was long. You hobbled out your horse, went coon or cat hunting with the boys or deer hunting if you so desired. But few people tried to make more money than needed to pay their debts. Land was a drug in the market at one dollar per acre, and all the old settlers were land poor.

I can better explain the faith people had in each other by telling you a tale. One day a man rode up to Uncle Add Lawrence's place on a tired horse and asked if it was here Mr. Lawrence lived. "That's me," said Uncle Add. The stranger stated that he lived in Houston County near Crockett, that while in San Antonio he got a message that his wife was very sick at home. He stated that he had started at once, but that his horse had failed and that he wanted to swap for a horse that would carry him home.

Uncle Add ordered Wesley, one of his sons, to drive up the saddle horses. On their arrival, Uncle Add told the man to pick out the horse that he wanted. When the selection was made, he asked Uncle Add how he would trade. The answer was give me ten dollars to boot. The man said, "That breaks the trade, for I have not got ten dollars."

"No," said Uncle Add, "go ahead, and send me the ten when you can." So he changed horses and rode away east in a long trot. After he was gone I asked the man's name. Uncle Add said, "I have never seed the man before." Said I, "Don't you think you have lost ten dollars?" "Naw," said he, "I'll get the money some of these days." Sure enough about a month afterward a man rode up and asked if here was where Mr. Add Lawrence lived. On being told that it was, he said that Mr. ────── who lived near Crockett asked him to come by and leave ten dollars that he owed in a horse trade. "Thar," said Uncle Add, "didn't I tell you I would git my money?"

But this country was not all Utopia or Arabia the Blessed. When you went out in the morning to get up your horse you had to watch your step or you would step on a centipede, tarantula, rattlesnake, or copperhead. Then when you sat down to eat breakfast, someone had to keep a brush going to keep away the flies; ticks and mosquitoes were present to vex you nearly the whole year. Ice when you needed it was unknown. In wet years, everybody had chills and fever for months.

Now for my tale. When the war began Old Man Banxton had a fine horse that I wanted to ride in the war. He asked one hundred dollars for him. He owed me fifty dollars for tuition and another neighbor owed me a like amount. I offered the two accounts for the horse, which proposition was accepted. Shortly afterward the party who was in debt to the old man skipped for Jackson County between suns, or ran away to keep from paying his debts. I will call him Smith, for that was not his name. When the old man heard that his debtor had skipped he loaded his double barreled shotgun, took his hobbles, a wallet of cornbread and meat, and went in hot pursuit, over-taking Smith a few miles below Bastrop. He cocked both bar-rels of his gun and yelled out halt. Smith sprang out of the wagon remarking, "Mr. Banxton, I forgot that little debt when I left, but here is a fifty dollar bill." The old man came home very jubilant. When he got his crop worked out, he told his boys Levi, Aaron, and Abner to saddle their ponies and they would go down to Frank Mundine's store at Lexington and trade out their fifty dollars.

On arrival he said to Mr. Mundine, "I want to trade fifty dollars' worth, and when I get that amount traded out, stop me, for I am such a fool that when I gets to buying goods I never know when to stop." After awhile Mundine said, "Mr. Banxton, your fifty dollars is out." The old man threw down his fifty dollar bill. Mr. Mundine laughed and remarked, "That is not money — not worth a cent." The old man pulled out a butcher knife and remarked, "Frank Mundine, I will cut your meat out if you fool me." Mundine stepped back and said, "That is a mustang liniment bill, and to show you that I am not trying to put up a job on you, here is a bottle of the same." Said the old man, "Put up them goods." "No," said Mundine, "take them home with you, for I know you are an honest man and will pay me when you get the money." "No," said the old man, "I pays for what I gets on the spot."

In the morning Levi came up to Uncle Add's and told the

tale. Uncle Add thought a minute and said, "Levi, whar's your pappy?"

"He's gone to Jackson County, starting before daylight, and he is awful mad." Uncle Add said to me, "Fell, git on your horse and ride over to Smith's brother Frank and tell him if he don't beat Old Man Banxton to Jackson County his brother will be shot down like he was an Indian."

Some days afterward the old man came home and told me he got the right sort of money this time. "Tell me all about it," said I. "Well, it took me some time after I got to Jackson County before I could find Smith's place. But when I found it I rode up, got down, threw my bridle reins over the picket fence, cocked both barrels of my gun, then hollered hello. Mrs. Smith came to the cabin door, her face as white as a sheet. I asked her whar was Smith. She said he was gone, 'but, Mr. Banxton, he left the right sort of money this time, and here it is.' She then handed me two twenty-dollar gold pieces and a ten-dollar gold piece. I said, 'Money is the end of the law,' and I let down the hammers of my gun and here I am."

After he had rested a few days he told Levi, Aaron, and Abner to saddle the ponies and go with him to Lexington after their goods. When he got there he threw the fifty dollars in gold on the counter and said to Mr. Mundine, "Is this mustang liniment money?"

Reminiscences of a Texas Pioneer

J. D. BRANTLEY

THE FOLLOWING TALES which my grandmother loved to tell are recorded, as nearly as possible, in her own words. Before her marriage, my grandmother was Sarah Jones Caroline Glimp. The story about the wild stallion is an event from her own childhood in DeWitt County. The panther story is about her father and his parents. Some of the members of the family say that the incident occurred in the early 1820's before the Glimp family left Tennessee, but Grandmother always insisted that it took place in East Texas during the late 1820's.

The Wild Stallion

In 1866 when Grandmother was a girl about nine or ten years old, the family lived in DeWitt County just north of Yorktown. At that time, the area was a rolling prairie dotted here and there with live oak clumps. Grass fires, sometimes started by the Indians who occasionally raided in that area, finally burned out all of the larger trees, and the land grew up in brush. One spring day her mother, Ardelia Woods Glimp, took Caroline and four younger children with her to visit the Woods family. The two homes were only a few miles apart, and the trip was accomplished easily with the swift bay mare that was used as the buggy horse. The visit was a long and pleasant one, and it was late afternoon before Ardelia loaded her family into the buggy and started home.

149

They had gone only a little way when Caroline noticed a great gray mustang stallion off to their right with a small band of mares. Realizing the possibility of trouble from the stallion, Ardelia slapped the bay mare's rump with the buggy reins sharply, with the intention of getting out of the mustang's vicinity.

Perhaps the wind carried the scent of the mare to the big stallion or perhaps he was at first only curious, but at the moment that the buggy began to move away from him more swiftly, he reared high, blasting a shrill challenge to the winds, and came thundering in pursuit. Caroline, at her mother's instructions, put the two youngest children in the front seat with their mother and took command of the back seat herself. Ardelia, in the meantime, stood upright in the buggy with feet braced apart and legs slightly bent at the knees—the way a man stands in a buggy; and, holding the reins in her left hand, she began to whip the bay mare harder with the extra length of reins in her right hand. The race was on.

Because of his sudden rush, the stallion quickly closed the distance between himself and the flying buggy, but he could never get quite close enough. Across the prairie they thundered for a good two miles or more, the mustang so close to the buggy that he almost seemed a part of it. Caroline had pushed the other children in the back seat to the floor and, at times, when the wild horse came closer and thrust out his head as if to bite, she slapped him with her "split" bonnet with all her might.

Seeing Caroline "hogging all the fun" made Mary Jane, the next eldest child, so unhappy that she could be reconciled only by joining Caroline on the back seat in combat with the horse. The animal followed them almost up to the home corral, Ardelia still standing and whipping the mare, and Caroline and Mary Jane banging the stallion's head with their bonnets. But when the buggy neared the house, the mustang gave up the chase and watched it draw up to the corral gate.

When Ardelia, with her tired and frightened children, finally

drew relaxed breath in the safety of home grounds, they saw
the huge gray shape stand silhouetted in the dusk on a little
rise and heard him give shrill vent to his hate before he disappeared below the horizon.

The Panther on the Roof

When my great-grandfather Glimp was a baby about three
months old, his parents and my great-great-grandfather Glimp's
brother went on a bear hunt. It was late fall, and they expected
to be gone from home for two or three weeks while they
secured a supply of winter meat.

Everything necessary for the trip was taken with them in
a two-wheeled cart with my grandmother Sarah and the baby
perched on top. When the little group reached the hunting
grounds, the men quickly threw up a makeshift hut about eight
or ten feet square with a clay-daubed chimney for the open
fireplace at one end. The first few days were spent in scouting
the immediate vicinity for game and in chopping immense
quantities of firewood for Sarah to use.

After a few days of exploration, the hunters decided that
at least one overnight hunting trip would be necessary, so,
carrying a great amount of firewood into the hut for Sarah
and leaving the hound with her for protection, the men set
out to find bear. During the afternoon of the first day, the
baby came down with colic. He was feverish and cross, and
he cried almost constantly. As dusk wore into night, Sarah,
alone and tired from worrying over her sick child, was suddenly
startled by an eerie scream far off in the night. It was the
blood-curdling cry of a panther.

Sarah threw another log on the low fire, even though the
night was not really cold, and kept trying to soothe the baby.
In a few minutes the panther screamed again, but this time
it was nearer. Trying to keep calm, Sarah began to walk the
floor with the baby, singing odd snatches of songs she remem-

bered hearing when she was a girl at home. But then the panther screamed a third time.

Sarah was no longer uneasy—she was frightened. The dog began to snarl and paw at the door; the baby cried; and Sarah threw another log on the fire. The pattern persisted. The mother's nervousness and the dog's ferocity were far from calming influences on the baby, who cried and sobbed with redoubled anguish. By this time the snarls of the great cat were heard in their own clearing. Sarah had a roaring fire in the fireplace, and the hound was throwing himself headlong against the door in a frenzy to attack a natural enemy. Then a long, dreadful silence fell around the hut. The silence was as horrible as the screams of the panther had been. Sarah heard a muffled thud above her head. Slowly she looked upward and saw the rafter poles bend slightly under the quiet tread of the panther.

Sarah felt numb, but she had no time to lose. Frantically she piled more wood on the fire, and, sensing that it might have been the baby's cries that drew the panther, the weary young mother talked and coaxed and walked with her small infant. She had given up trying to silence the dog, which had almost gone mad with rage when the panther jumped upon the roof. Suddenly the air was shattered by the panther's scream immediately over her head. She laid the baby down long enough to find the largest knife in the hut. She tested its sharpness with her thumb and then kept it with her as she went back to the baby on the pallet. While holding the still sobbing child, she began to take inventory of the supply of firewood. Comparing as best she could the amount that had been left with her and the amount now remaining in the stack by the fireplace, she realized that she had not been frugal with her only real protection. For, if the fire went out, the wide chimney would provide ample entryway for the panther.

She carefully looked around the room. There was no other wood except a chest and a box. The chest was a family heirloom; she would save it until the last. Her eyes were just returning to the pile of wood near the fireplace when her glance was involuntarily drawn upward.

The hot fire she had kept going in order to prevent the panther from entering through the chimney was causing the clay coating to crack. If the clay began to flake off, the chimney and the whole hut would catch on fire.

Sarah now plunged into one of those awful suspensions between two fears. At one time she felt that she had let the fire get too low and that the panther would be down before she could get it hotter, and at another time that the chimney was in flames. Twice she was sure she heard the panther sniffing around the chimney opening. By the sagging of the rafter poles, she watched his movements as he paced over the roof and then, after a long while, when she thought she had lost track of his position on the roof, she heard his cry a little distance from the hut. It was only then that Sarah realized that the baby had stopped crying.

Laying the sleeping infant on the pallet, Sarah, her knees shaking with relief and exhaustion, moved closer to the fire and drew the dog to her in order to quiet him. Her only fear now was that his growling would waken the baby or that she would go to sleep and let the fire go out.

Morning found her still awake before the fire, but she must have dozed after daylight, for she was roused by the hound's eager whining and the sound of her husband pounding on the barred door.

Taking the dog, the men trailed the panther and found him asleep on a great branch of a tree scarcely a hundred yards from the cabin. There was no panther skin memento. The hound, usually very obedient, jumped upon the body of the animal, which fell dead at the first shot, and could not be pulled off until after he had literally ripped and chewed the cat beyond recognition. It is doubtful that Sarah would have wanted any reminders of that night anyhow.

Around the Fire with My Abuelitos

GUADALUPE DUARTE

WHEN I was a child I lived for some time with my grandparents in Laredo. My abuelo was around sixty-five years old, but he still retained the well-developed body of his youthful years. His eyes carried the green of the Spaniards even though his ancestry included plenty of Indian blood. My abuela was rather stout and her eyes had lost the shining coal color that fades with youth.

As we sat around the fire after sundown my abuelitos would tell me stories that had been passed down from generation to generation. Right after supper I would crowd in between the two and listen until I was sent to bed. One night my abuelo began this way.

"En aquel tiempo your abuela and I lived in an old, old house on top of a hill. We had been hearing strange noises at night in the kitchen, but had not paid much attention to them. One night they were especially loud, and I got up to see what was the matter. These noises always came from underneath our big black wood stove.

"The stove seemed to be dancing 'La Cucaracha.' It was jumping here and there and twirling and twirling around. But this lasted only a few minutes, and as soon as the clock had struck twelve everything grew quiet again.

"I made up my mind then and there to tell my compadre about the whole thing. Compadre Sebastián knew about these things better than anyone else in the whole country.

" 'Le pegamos al clavo,' said my compadre. 'This is beyond doubt a ghost who wishes to give us a fortune if we will pay off the debts that he owed in his earthly life.' A ghost can never rest, he said, until all his debts have been paid on earth. Whoever dug up the money buried under our black stove would be muy rico, but he must repay the ghost's debts or forfeit the fortune and his life too.

"That night my compadre and I began to dig under the stove. 'Ay, Dios mío, Dios mío,' your abuela kept exclaiming, 'The Lord will surely punish you for this, Miguel.' 'Keep quiet, María,' I would tell her, as I scooped up another shovelful of dirt.

"Suddenly the earth began to tremble, and a frightful voice was heard above the trembling—'Quien toma mi fortuna, toma mis duedas también!' Whoever takes my fortune takes my debts too! My compadre and I decided to have a few swallows of mescal before digging again. Mescal does things for you. Soon we had uncovered a heavy old chest. We took up the chest and placed it on our kitchen floor. And, look, the chest was full of gold coins. My compadre and I split the gold in half because of his advice and help. Compadre Sebastián took his half in the old chest. We agreed that each of us would give half of the money needed to pay off the spirit's debts, and Sebastián took my part with him, promising to see that all debts were settled.

"A week passed and I was still planning what to buy with my half of the fortune. One day my thoughts were interrupted by some excitement outside the house. My neighbor came running in, shouting, 'Something has happened to your compadre Sebastián! Come quickly!'

"As fast as I could, I ran to my compadre's house. When I got there, a crowd of neighbors had already gathered outside. From the murmurings of the crowd I concluded that my compadre would not be able to spend the gold that we had found. When I entered the door the first thing that caught my eye was the body of Sebastián on his bed. Between sobs his wife told me what had happened. It seems that compadre Sebastián had not paid off the debts of the ghost and because of this his life and gold were taken. Instead of gold coins, the chest now held filthy black mud. Sebastián's mouth was covered with mud. Someone in the crowd said that he had been witness to another of these deaths—the ghost had probably stuffed Sebastián's mouth with the gold that he was keeping all for himself and later this gold had turned into mud.

"Feeling very sorry for my compadre, I walked away almost without bidding his widow goodbye. I was anxious to find out what had happened to my part of the fortune. In the front yard your abuela was waiting for me. There were tears in her eyes, but somehow I knew that they were tears of gladness. Taking her by the hand, I went immediately to the place where the gold was hidden. All that was left of it was a pile of the same kind of mud that was found in the chest. 'Miguel,' your abuela said, 'God has been good to us. He spared our lives.'"

Placing her hand affectionately on my head, my abuela scolded my abuelo for telling such a horrible ghost story. Then she began a story of her own about the pavo real or peacock and how it came to have the beautiful feathers it now has.

"The pavo real used to be a very, very proud bird because its feathers were colored bright red and yellow. At that time all of the other birds had plain gray or black feathers. Everywhere he went the peacock boasted of the brightness and beauty of the colors adorning him. The bird that he ridiculed most was the cuervo or crow. The pavo was forever taunting the cuervo because of the cuervo's ugly black feathers. Finally in desperation the cuervo decided to leave the country and settle somewhere else.

"He packed his few belongings and flew off toward other lands. Now the pavo, like everybody else, loved to take a nap right after dinner, and as the cuervo flew along he looked down and saw the pavo asleep. 'Ah, Señor Pavo, now I shall have my revenge,' said the cuervo. He glided down to where the pavo was sleeping, and taking clay of all colors from the banks of a near-by creek, he set about coloring the pavo in ridiculous patterns. When the pavo awoke, the clay had hardened and he could not take it off. After seeing himself in the waters of a creek, Señor Pavo Real decided to go into hiding. One day he could not endure it any longer and had to come out to look for food. When Señor Cuervo saw him, he began to laugh and shout at the top of his voice. All the birds flew from their trees to see the novelty. But when Señor Tecolote saw what was the matter, he commanded everyone to stop laughing. Since they all respected his judgment and authority, they obeyed.

" 'I am sorry for every time that I have laughed at you,' the pavo said. 'I promise that if you restore my color I will never again make fun of anyone.' The birds took pity on the poor pavo and decided to help him. At the direction of the owl, all the birds pitched in to help design some pretty colors for Señor Pavo. They designed so well that to this day the pavo real is the world's most beautiful bird, but at the same time he is the most modest."

Now it was my abuelo's turn.

"Speaking of a cuervo," he began, "let me tell you a funny story of a crow that my padre used to tell me. There was once an old Mexican peon who would walk all the way from Mexico City to Monterrey. One time when he arrived in Monterrey, his friend's house already had visitors, and not being a person to inconvenience others, the old man declared that he would go somewhere else. 'Well,' the old man's amigo said, 'why don't you go to Juan Pérez' house? I know him very well and you can tell him that I sent you. He is a very nice fellow, and I know that he will give you posada.' Old Joaquín decided to do just that. It looked like rain and he wanted to have shelter somewhere. As he arrived at the house of Juan Pérez the rain

began to come down in torrents. Joaquín knocked on the door
and a harsh voice called out, 'Quién es? Qué quiere?' 'It is I,
Joaquín,' the old man answered. 'Your compadre said that you
might have some room here for me. Open the door please and
let me in or I will surely catch pneumonia out here.'

"'Quién es? Qué quiere?' the harsh voice asked again.
Joaquín repeated his plea and the harsh voice asked the same
two questions as before. After about fifteen minutes of this,
Joaquín gave up hope. 'And my friend said that this Juan
Pérez was a very nice man! Here he is joking with me while I
am freezing out here in the rain,' thought old Joaquín. 'If you
don't mind, I'll sleep out here beside the door!' shouted Joaquín
to the voice inside.

"In the morning when the owner of the house opened his
door he found Joaquín half-frozen and wet to the bone. 'Come
in, come in, my good man! Why didn't you call me before you
got all wet?' asked Juan Pérez. 'He no doubt is making jest of
what happened,' thought Joaquín. But as he entered the house
he heard the same two questions—'Quién es? Qué quiere?'—in
the same harsh voice. Turning around to see who it was, he
saw a huge black crow mimicking a human voice."

My abuelitos both wanted to send me off to bed, but I
pleaded with them to tell just one more story. My abuela, not
to be outdone by my abuelo, started one of her tales.

"There used to live in the mountains near Monterrey a man
who boasted of curing everything under the sun. One day he
was brought a patient who was very ill, and upon seeing this
man the curandero promised to drive out the sickness within
a few days. 'The huisache tree will cure anything,' claimed the
curandero.

"On the first day the curandero tried boiled leaves of
huisache, but the patient got worse. 'I'll try stewed twigs of
huisache and they will surely cure him,' cried the curandero.
The next day the poor sick man had to swallow about a liter
of stewed twigs, but he felt no better.

"The third day the man looked as if he would die at any minute, but this did not worry the curandero. He now tried cooked bark of huisache, but this didn't cure the sick man either. 'There is only one thing that will surely cure him,' said the curandero. 'And this is the heart of the huisache.'"

My grandmother paused there and said to me, "Lupe, let this be a lesson to you." Then she continued, "On the fourth day the sick man was fed raw huisache heart. And, look, the curandero did away not only with the huisache tree, but also with the sick man!"

And with that I was sent off to bed.

Russell Tales

MAURITA RUSSELL LUEG

WHEN PEOPLE live on the soil for a long time it becomes a part of them. Their amusements as well as their working hours are influenced by it. Superstition mingles with love of the land to give rise to many fascinating tales. For generations children have sat staring, with mouths open, at a mother or father telling some tale that gave an aspect of wonder to a familiar landmark.

For six generations the Russell family has tilled the soil of the old home place near West, north of Waco. Although much acreage of the original ranch has passed from their hands through the years, the site of the old homestead still belongs to one of the Russell boys. As time has gone by, the land has produced many legends that are proudly related by the family and neighbors. Some of these stories are made up of truth, some are made of pure fancy, and others are a pleasant mixture of both.

James Henry Russell, his wife Eva Marie, and their six children came to Texas from Maryland. The family settled on an expanse of rolling prairie northeast of the spot where the town of West is now located. At the time of their arrival West did not exist. The closest settlement was some twelve miles away; it was a small cluster of homes called Bold Springs. The settlers lived in dugouts covered with sod.

The waves of black prairie rolled gently as far as the eye could see; not a tree dotted the landscape. Although an abundance of scrub mesquite and hackberry grows in this area now, old-timers avow that this was not always true. The grass was lush and plentiful, but fresh water was scarce. James Henry built a home for his family on the crest of a small hill overlooking a shallow valley. The new home had everything that could be desired except drinking water, which had to be hauled several miles from a spring. This spring is now called Bennett Springs.

As the years passed, cattle raising and farming prospered—and so did the Russells. James Henry and Eva Marie added eight more children to the six brought from Maryland, and their first child, a girl, made them grandparents. Early one spring morning, the oldest Russell boy came riding up to the house at a breakneck pace. He breathlessly told his father that a large number of their cattle were missing and that the signs showed they had been driven off by a group of men. James Henry, his son, and his son-in-law set out at once to overtake the thieves. One of the other children was sent to get help from the neighboring settlers.

That afternoon when the posse arrived to assist the three men, it was too late. They were dead. The Russells had caught up with the cattle thieves just a short distance from Bennett Springs. In a gun battle six of the rustlers were killed along with the three pursuers. All of the guns were empty except one. The gun held cocked in James Henry's dead hand had one shell left.

The bodies of the Russell men were taken home and buried close to their house. When Eva Marie was given her husband's gun, she placed it above the door. The family grew up and gradually scattered, but the gun remained untouched. The writer's father heard about the weapon as a child. When he grew up, he searched for and found the gun in the ruins of the old house. It was an old cap-and-ball, rusted in the position in which it had been left—cocked.

Many years later a friend of the Russells made a business

trip to Maryland. While there he met an old man on a park
bench. The old man, upon discovering that the traveler was
from West, asked if he knew the Russells. The answer was,
"Yes, quite well." The old man then told this story: When a
young boy he had joined a group of rustlers. On their first
job they had raided the Russell herd. Feeling that their theft
would not be noticed for several days, they stopped for a
leisurely dinner at Bennett Springs. Just as they were finishing
their meal, they were discovered by the Russells. A bitter gun
fight followed. This man was the only survivor. He had been
wounded in the arm. For weeks he hid out in the river bottom,
living on roots and berries. When he grew strong enough to
travel he headed north and stayed there.

Happy in their choice of a homesite, the Russells felt
there was but one serious drawback, and that was the inconvenience of hauling drinking water several times a week. Much
was said but nothing was done about the problem until Abe,
James Henry's youngest son, grew into manhood. Abe was
determined to find water close to the house. He sent for
drillers to come and dig a well. Several came but they all said
the same thing: there was not any water there; it would be a
waste of time and money to drill. Grasping at straws, Abe
finally sent for an old prospector who searched for water and
minerals with a "witching stick." Everyone laughed at the
idea of ever finding anything that way. Abe and the old man
were confident, however, and the two spent hours walking over
the area, Abe eager and hopeful and the old man holding the
willow stick in his hands. A few hundred yards from the
house, in the bottom of the shallow valley, the stick pulled out
of the man's hand. The two began to dig. At three feet they
hit water, an underground spring. Here was an abundance of
fresh sweet water. Once released, the spring continued to flow
until it made a pond, and then gradually it became a creek
winding along the floor of the valley. Only during the severest
years of the recent drought did this creek cease flowing, and

even then, although but a trickle, the spring continued to issue forth.

The valley through which the creek ran, the Russells believed, was the location of an old Indian battleground. The abundance of arrowheads in the vicinity seems to substantiate the story. Children of the family have often gathered them by the pocketful. As the story has it, one of the chiefs was killed in the exact spot where the spring was discovered.

About two years after the creek had developed, the settlers began to wonder if perhaps the old chief and his warriors were not showing their resentment against the white men who had so brazenly disturbed their peaceful slumber. One night after a heavy rain a young farm hand saw something strange on the bank of the creek. He described it as about the size of a dog; he said it was pale and shiny, alive but somehow not quite real. Too frightened to move at first, he watched this ghostly being for some time. It would appear on the bank of the creek, right at the water's edge, then would float along the course of the water for a short distance only to veer away from the creek bed and disappear. Suddenly it would be back where it started. News of the strange apparition spread rapidly. After that it was quite common for the ghost to be seen after a heavy rain, and only after such a rain. Most of the people firmly believed that it was the resentful spirit of some dead Indian.

This spirit was even known to follow men on horseback for several yards. While they were riding along the watercourse it would suddenly appear at their side. Spurring their horses, they found that it would remain close to their heels for a distance and then disappear.

Today this frightening ghost has been logically explained. In the soil over which the water cut its channel were deposits of phosphorus. The water washed away the covering and thus released a gas. These balls of gas are especially noticeable after a heavy rain because as new portions of the bank are cut away more of the phosphorus is exposed. As a child the writer often saw the little glowing dots left in the tracks of cattle as they crossed the stream.

A family cemetery grew up on the spot where the three Russell men who had been killed by the rustlers were buried. As years passed, neighbors buried their dead there also. Eventually the plot of land on which the cemetery was located was deeded to the public. It was named Liberty Grove. One dark autumn night it was the scene of a tragic accident.

When the writer's great-grandmother was a young girl in her early teens, she attended a slumber party given by one of the neighbors, at which about ten girls were present. Even in those days none of the guests slept at a slumber party. As the night wore on, the conversation turned to ghosts, ghost stories, and cemeteries. All but one girl admitted that they would be afraid to go to a cemetery at night. The one girl held fast to her boast that she was afraid of nothing, not even ghosts. The other girls called her bluff and double-dared her to go to the Liberty Grove cemetery, which was about a mile and a half away. She took the dare; and to prove that she had fulfilled her mission, she was to take a knife and stick it in the grave of a person they all knew who had recently passed on. She took the knife and slipped out of the house.

Next morning she was found stretched across the grave, her face frozen in an expression of terror. The hem of her skirt was pinned to the grave by the knife.

While still in its infancy, the settlement at Bold Springs was wiped out in an Indian attack. Every man, woman, and child was killed and heads, arms, and legs were severed from their bodies.

On the anniversary of this massacre a headless horseman is supposed to ride. It is believed that he is the spirit of one of the Bold Springs settlers riding in a desperate effort to warn the Russell ranch of the Indian attack.

Many persons have heard the sound of his stallion's hoof-beats as he rode up the road in front of the house. Many colored people have actually seen him, the headless body hunched over the horse's neck, plying quirt and spur, pushing the horse to the utmost. The magnificent white stallion races like the wind, striking sparks from his hooves and breathing fire from his mouth.

Once these stories became current it was impossible to get a colored person to travel the road in front of the Russell house at night on the date that the headless horseman was supposed to ride.

For years Negroes from the surrounding countryside have fished in the Russell Creek. The writer remembers one old Negro woman who often told of seeing a ghost not far from the banks, something more definite than a pale ball of light. One afternoon the woman and her husband had had especially good luck at fishing. They did not notice the time and were caught in the creek bed after dark. Frightened by all the stories of spirits which they had heard about the place, they were hurrying toward the road as fast as their feet would carry them. About a hundred yards from the road, the couple saw a white, transparent man. The ghost tried to tell them something but was unable to speak. After a few moments of gesturing wildly, the ghost vanished. Thoroughly frightened, the couple ran all the way home. A short while later the woman's brother was killed in an accident. The Negro woman firmly believes that the ghost she and her husband saw was the spirit of her father, trying to warn them of the brother's approaching doom.

Unguarded by a ghost, a treasure lies buried somewhere on land that belongs or once belonged to the Russells. During the Civil War a band of Union soldiers made a raid on the Russell farm. Seeing the men riding across the prairie, the lady of the house hastily hid everything of value. The only object hid with caution was her jewel box. It is said to have contained diamonds, rubies, emeralds, and a strand of pearls. The lady had come from a very wealthy family and these were the only reminders she had of her background. The Union soldiers were looking for food, however, and they made no search for valuables. After the soldiers had gone the children restored everything to its proper place. For some reason the mother did not retrieve her jewel box. Not too many days later, she was taken seriously ill and passed on. When the family tried to find the missing treasure they were unable to do so. Its general vicinity was known, but no one has ever discovered the exact location. Many, including outsiders, have looked for the buried jewels; but their whereabouts remains a secret.

These are the stories that the writer has heard time and time again concerning the farm on which she grew up. How much is true and how much is fanciful are questions that she never asked when as a child she sat in front of a roaring fire on a cold winter night listening with awe and wonder.

Contributors

RILEY AIKEN's fine collection published in *Puro Mexicano* (1935) as "A Pack Load of Mexican Tales" is not likely to be forgotten. Mr. Aiken grew up on the Texas-Mexican border and has traveled extensively in Mexico in search of tales. He teaches modern languages in the Kansas State College at Emporia.

MODY C. BOATRIGHT is secretary and editor of the Texas Folklore Society. At the University of Texas he conducts a seminar in the literature of the Southwest. *Folk Laughter on the American Frontier* (1949) is one of his books.

J. D. BRANTLEY teaches at Southwest Texas State College in San Marcos and at the same time continues his graduate studies at the University of Texas. In a seminar taken in the summer of 1957 he was encouraged to write down the two family tales that appear in this book.

REIDAR TH. CHRISTIANSEN is professor emeritus of folklore at the University of Oslo. He is one of the leading folklorists now at work. Among his books are *The Vikings and the Viking Wars in Irish and Gaelic Tradition* (Oslo, 1931) and *The Dead and the Living* (Oslo, 1946). In 1956-57 he was a visiting lecturer at the University of Indiana. In April, 1957, he came to Texas to deliver lectures in Austin and Dallas.

During his twenty years of editorship J. FRANK DOBIE saw the Texas Folklore Society firmly established and its publications take an honored place in the literature of folklore. Besides the publications that he has edited, he has written a dozen or so books, all well known to members of the Society—*Tales of Old-Time Texas* (1955) being the latest.

GUADALUPE DUARTE was born in Laredo and attended school there. After graduating from Laredo Junior College he entered the University of Texas. While taking the course in Life and Literature of the Southwest he wrote down the folktales contributed to this book. He is now in the U.S. Navy, attached to the Public Information Office.

LANVIL GILBERT is at present a graduate student at the University of Texas. In the spring of 1957 he took a course in the literature of the Southwest and in the summer he enrolled in a graduate seminar, in which he wrote the article printed here.

EVERETT A. GILLIS is a teacher of English at Texas Technological College. In 1948 he received the doctor's degree at the University of Texas. He is a publishing poet as well as a teacher.

HOWARD C. KEY was trained in meteorology during World War II and served as a weather officer. He teaches English at North Texas State College. A summary of the paper printed in this book was sent out by the wire services, with the result that Mr. Key received many letters about tornadoes from all over the United States and several foreign countries.

MAURITA RUSSELL LUEG was encouraged to write the "family saga" of the Russells of West while she was taking Life and Literature of the Southwest at the University of Texas in 1957. Since graduating she has been teaching English at Taylor, though she still lives in Austin. Russell was her maiden name.

ELTON MILES teaches English at Sul Ross State College and collects folklore in the Big Bend. He has contributed articles on this subject to previous publications of the Texas Folklore

Society. Recently he edited the memoirs of Will Tom Carpenter, a Texas cattleman, for the University of Texas Press.

AMÉRICO PAREDES grew up in Brownsville, where he once worked on a Spanish language newspaper. He has received three degrees from the University of Texas, where he wrote his doctoral dissertation on Gregorio Cortez, noted ballad hero; his book on Cortez is due for publication soon. He is now teaching English at Texas Western College.

JIM ROWDEN was graduated from the University of Texas in 1957. The two oil stories printed here were submitted as part of his term paper in Life and Literature of the Southwest, a course originated by J. Frank Dobie in 1929.

F. S. WADE (1836-1925) was born in Canada and came to the United States early in life. Information about his youthful days is not plentiful, but it is known that he served in the Confederate army and was later addressed as "Captain Wade." He made a study of the Confederacy and built up a good collection of books and papers on the subject. The stories published in the Elgin newspaper are evidently from a MS which Captain Wade left at his death, "Add Lawrence's Tales of Early Days in Texas." The first half of this MS has been located, but not the second half.